Everett Kircher
Michigan's Resort Pioneer

Edited and Published by Stephen Janisse and Robert Vincent

Vincent and Associates Bloomfield Hills, Michigan

This is the story of Boyne USA – as told by Everett Kircher. Special thanks is given to the late William Winchester for the research he compiled and to Boyne's Stephen Kircher, Art Tebo and Nancy Magnus for their untiring efforts to keep this project moving forward. In addition, we thank David Patritto and Kristin Blumreich at Colorforms Art Studio for the design and layout of this book.

This book is dedicated to my wife, Lois; to my children, John, Amy, Stephen and Kathryn; and to my parents, who taught me the solid Republican values that I live by and fiercely preach. I also want to acknowledge the contributions to the success of Boyne by many. Notably to Charles "Chuck" Moll, my general manager, who worked with me for nearly 40 years; to Victor Gottschalk, my first instructor and Boyne's first director of skiing; to Stein Eriksen and Othmar Schneider, Olympic gold medal winners who first brought the modern method of skiing to Boyne; to Boyne employees, who helped the company grow and prosper; to America – to the officers and directors of companies and associations who brought their groups to Boyne properties for meetings and conventions; and to many, many other friends and associates, including that hardy, leather-boot, bear-trap-binding bunch of early skiers who skied with me and helped popularize the sport and patronized Boyne Mountain.

Everett Kircher, 1998

Othmar Schneider was an Olympic Gold Medal winner in 1952. After considerable coaxing, he agreed to become the director of the ski school at Boyne Mountain and spent fourteen years in that role.

Thoughts by Othmar Schneider

Certainly my years at Boyne Mountain with Everett Kircher were most enjoyable in many ways. Who would have ever thought after growing up in the Austrian Alps and winning a gold medal at the 1952 Olympics, I would spend 14 winters as the director of a ski school at a ski resort with a vertical drop of 500 feet.

It was Everett's vision and his tenacity to send his general manager Chuck Moll to Portillo, Chile to try to convince me to come to Michigan. After many phone calls I agreed to come to Boyne Mountain.

Once at Boyne it did not take me long to get caught up in Everett's excitement, to help make Boyne the ski center of the Midwest. With major metropolitan areas within driving distance of Boyne, we had a large number of skiers that we could expose to the best snow making and grooming in the Midwest. It was not only his genius in developing many patents for snow making but also his revolutionary ideas for ski lifts.

Over the years I have had great admiration for Everett's understanding of how much a successful ski school contributes to the success of a ski resort. His keen interest in ski techniques made Everett an expert skier and made him realize the Austrian method could make Boyne one of the leading ski centers in America. Thousands of skiers came and enjoyed Boyne's hospitality and great skiing.

On this 50th anniversary of Boyne USA I want to add my best wishes to Everett and his family, and to the great success they have achieved.

Table of Contents

Boyne Mountain circa 1993

1st hole on Links golf course at Bay Harbor G.C.

Forward By Art Tebo

There is a popular cliché – "He marches to a different drum." In my thirty plus years working beside Everett, I have witnessed this "different" march. I've experienced some frustration at times, but mainly have marveled at his accomplishments.

Everett possesses an exceptional ability to concentrate on a given subject, idea or concept and not let anyone or anything interfere with his thought process. For example, on a typical busy Saturday at Boyne Mountain, I may poke my head into Everett's office and say to him, "I would like to finish talking about the possibility of income averaging on lift tickets." He says, "O.K., let's go to lunch."

We will walk from the administration offices to the main lodge for lunch. We always seem to encounter several different groups of people who say "hi" to Mr. K. and/or myself. I generally will acknowledge them by saying, "Hi, nice to see you," however there is no response from Everett.

Often while we are trying to eat and discuss business, more people will come up to say hello, wish us well, or talk about skiing conditions. Again, there is little or no response from Everett. Late in the afternoon when I again see those same people away from Everett, they might say, "Is Mr. K. mad at me? Why didn't he acknowledge me when I said hello to him today?" I generally advise them that he probably never heard them. Everett was totally absorbed with the subject at hand, in this case, income averaging on lift tickets. From the time we left his office, sat down for lunch, ordered, ate our meal and completed our discussion, he was so deep in thought on income averaging that he was totally unaware of the various acknowledgments of people. When I started his mind moving on the subject, everything else was pushed aside. This is part of the insatiable thirst for knowledge and background information which is integral to Everett's analysis process.

Everett can quickly digest and analyze the information you give him. Don't be surprised however, when he uses that same information to reinforce his point of view or attempt to win you over to his position. He may accept your information as factual, but will then use it to help support his own particular position. If indeed your position is opposite you will have to stand your ground and fight hard to prevail. In addition, you must remember that many months from now he is liable to bring up that conversation and he will remember everything you had to say. Again, a testimonial to his power of concentration. His alleged "aloofness" for years can be attributed to his tremendous power of concentration, and in no way should be interpreted as a deliberate snub.

Everett has always possessed a fascination with what makes a given product or gadget work. He is a student of engineering concepts and Boyne would definitely not be where it is today without his mechanical ingenuity. I think of him as Boyne's personal mechanical engineer. He loves to buy a thing-a-ma-jig, as we say in northern Michigan, and proceed to take it apart and put it back together in an attempt to make it better. More often than not, he is successful. Many times he will take a given product apart such as a fishing rod, a shot gun, or something else that has not worked properly for a long time, and within minutes have it working again better than ever. This shows Everett's confidence in his ability to outthink and outperform others. This confidence has been demonstrated in countless situations over the years as he has taken concepts and ideas that have been moderately successful for others, adopted parts or all of those ideas and gone on to make them hugely successful.

Everett always wants to take something that is good and make it better. He has been motivated for many years to develop the best skiing and skiing conditions possible. This has come out of his personal experience. He wrote the book on the design and engineering concepts for modern ski lifts.

Early on, Everett would take long treks to Sun Valley, Idaho, and then later, when Boyne was established, to other parts of America and Europe, borrow the best skiing ideas and then improve on them. This has again been demonstrated on numerous occasions as Everett perfected ski lift concepts, ski school techniques and snow-making capabilities to make Boyne properties the envy of the skiing world.

Early on, when Everett realized that you could not always count on Mother Nature to provide good snow for skiing, he began researching the possibility of making snow. He read about other's ideas in this area, studied the patents and eventually formulated a system he could create himself – the Boyne Snow Machine. Needless to say, this snow-making capability has made an enormous difference in the success of all Boyne ski properties.

Everett's success over the years can also be attributed to his early experience in life and his hard work ethic. Born in St. Louis, Missouri in 1916, Everett moved to Detroit at three months old, lived through some lean years, and witnessed the $5.00 a day influence of Henry Ford.

His experiences with his own machine shops and auto dealerships greatly influenced his attitudes and convictions. These beliefs dictated how he should later build, operate and maintain his ski areas. This strong work ethic has led Everett to surround himself with people who believe likewise.

Throughout the years, we have been able to make Boyne U.S.A. Resorts among the best ski and golf facilities in the country. This has taken constant care and investment in each facility. Every year we must invest in more and better lift capabilities, better grooming and better accommodations. Such has always been the case and maybe always will be. Fortunately, as those investments are made, the properties appreciate in value and that represents the eventual payoff.

Technology has enabled us to continuously improve our lift capabilities to answer the demand. Developing the first four place chairlift and the first high-speed six place lift has also enhanced Boyne's reputation and capabilities.

All of our experience has helped greatly as we venture further with the purchases of Brighton Ski Resort outside Salt Lake City, Utah and Crystal Mountain outside Seattle, Washington. These additions expand Boyne, U.S.A.'s skiing potential to over 1.5 million customers a year.

Boyne U.S.A. Resorts will continue to grow beyond this, our 50th year. Everett's four children are the majority shareholders in the company, therefore it's their future. Their interests, like their father's, are to continue to develop unparalleled skiing and golf experiences.

Bay Harbor G.C., our most recent venture, that Everett's son Steve and I have spent a good part of the last two years overseeing, has been compared to Pebble Beach in terms of a golf experience. It promises to rival anything in the country and will certainly be the best in the Midwest.

Everett, at 81 years of age, remains active today. His sheer will and determination serve as a wonderful example of how the rest of us, including his four kids, plan and execute the future of Boyne U.S.A. Resorts.

Introducing Kircher

"I'd rather be known as a great fly fisherman."

While Everett F. Kircher is acknowledged as one of the best in the world at dropping a dry fly on the nose of a trout, his true claim to fame is in the sport of snow skiing.

He parlayed a modest 500-foot mountain in the Midwest into one of the largest individually owned resort empires in the world, and amassed a sizable fortune along the route.

His company, Boyne USA Resorts, of which Kircher is founder and active president, consists of five major ski and summer resorts: Boyne Mountain and Boyne Highlands, Big Sky of Montana (originally founded by the late Chet Huntley in 1970), Brighton Ski Bowl in Big Cottonwood Canyon near Salt Lake City, Utah and Crystal Mountain in Seattle, Washington. Boyne USA also owns and operates a scenic chairlift in Gatlinburg, Tennessee and ten golf courses from Montana to Florida.

Kircher started skiing when downhill was a brand new sport in North America. He skied Sun Valley shortly after it opened, vacationed there for 13 successive winters, and once won the prestigious downhill Gold Sun Race. Since then he has skied at major areas around the world until a stroke took him off the boards.

In 1947, with two fellow skiers, he started Boyne Mountain in Michigan. He purchased a used, single-person chairlift from Sun Valley, the first chairlift ever built in the world, and had it shipped to his fledgling resort. Knowing that uphill transportation was the key to success, he converted that single chair to a double in his Detroit Studebaker auto dealership.

Defying the advice of chairlift "experts," he installed the world's first triple chair at Boyne Highlands in 1963, following it with the first-ever four-place chairlift at Boyne Mountain in 1965. This four-place was such an innovation that the executives from Doppelmayr, the giant Austria-based manufacturer of trams and lifts, visited Boyne to see how it was designed.

In 1990 he installed the Midwest's first high-speed detachable quad at Boyne Highlands. He notched another milestone, erecting the first detachable six-place chairlift in the United States at the Mountain.

Kircher's ski innovations included pioneering artificial snowmaking and co-inventing the Boyne Snowmaker, the first efficient device accepted as the standard for marginal temperature snowmaking. He patented the snowmaker which is currently in use around the world. Kircher was also at the forefront of many of the grooming techniques and much of the equipment used today, including the first snow tiller in 1965.

His interest in skiing technique resulted in bringing Olympic gold-medal winner Stein Eriksen to Boyne Mountain to head the ski school and teach the "reverse shoulder" method that the young, hot-shot racers were using. Later, when Eriksen decided to move to the Rockies, Everett hired Othmar Schneider, also an Olympic champion. When most of the world was teaching the up-down-and-around Arlberg technique, Boyne skiers were already mastering this counter-rotation method. In the fifties and early sixties, Boyne skiers were easily recognized and emulated wherever they skied.

As the ski business prospered, Kircher became aware of the need to fill rooms and keep his employees on staff during the warm weather months. A friend suggested golf as a drawing card. Using his father's ancient farm tractor, he carved out a sporty 9-hole layout at the base of the Boyne Mountain lodge.

After acquiring a local ski area in nearby Harbor Springs, and developing the ski facilities, Kircher got into golf seriously. He hired famed architect Robert Trent Jones, Sr. to design an 18-hole layout at the newly named Boyne Highlands Resort. The Heather course was dedicated in 1968 and by 1971 was listed in Golf Digest's Top 100 courses in the U.S. The Heather was the spark that ignited the golf boom in Northwest Michigan, now referred to as "America's Summer Golf Capital." Boyne USA has continued this "boom" with the addition of the prestigious Bay Harbor Golf Club near Petoskey, Michigan. This course offers several challenging holes that run atop a bluff high above the shores of Lake Michigan.

Kircher's interests aren't limited to ski and golf resorts. He is a jet pilot and an avid sportsman, traveling the globe in his Citation jet to fish the waters of Scotland, Iceland, Labrador, Canada, Russia and the U.S. In 1967, he caught a 47-pound Atlantic salmon on an artificial fly in the Alta River in Norway. In 1985, he caught and released a 53 and 55 pound trophy salmon in the Restigouche River in New Brunswick, Canada all in the span of one week. His love for the wily salmon prompted him to plant 25,000 salmon fingerlings in the Boyne River, a freshwater stream that fronts his Michigan home.

He has also hunted a variety of game, including chamois in Austria, antelope in Wyoming, elk in Montana, leopard and elephant and other big game in Africa, dove in the

Baja Peninsula and wildfowl in Mexico, Denmark, Canada and the United States.

In 1953, aided by his father John Kircher, he engineered and erected a scenic chair-lift in Gatlinburg, Tennessee, at the foot of the Great Smoky Mountains National Park. It turned out to be a cash cow, financing much of the expansion of Boyne Mountain. The income from Gatlinburg paid for many Michigan skiers lift tickets.

Plaques honoring Kircher adorn his office walls, but leave him unimpressed. The one he laughs and points to most frequently is the one that proclaims: "He who dies with the most toys wins."

Born in 1916 in St. Louis, Missouri, Kircher was an infant when his father was lured to Detroit to work for Ford Motor for $5 per day. He attended public schools in Detroit, and attended the University of Michigan. Prior to getting into the ski business, he sold mobile homes and owned Chrysler and Studebaker auto dealerships.

Kircher lives with his wife, Lois, in Boyne Falls. His son, John, manages Boyne's western operations; daughter Amy, manages the Boyne South golf course in Naples, Florida; son, Stephen, oversees and directs most of the Michigan operations; and Kathryn, youngest of the four, manages Boyne Design Group which sees to the ongoing task of decorating, updating and refurbishing the Boyne USA hotels, lodges and condos, plus all the interior design work at the Bay Harbor Golf Club, Yacht Club and the elegant Inn at Bay Harbor.

Everett Kircher is a self-made man of extraordinary vision who grew up determined to "be somebody." He will be remembered for his lasting contributions to Alpine skiing, golf and to the economy of northern Michigan.

Following is his story, as told through his words. They convey the values he preaches and lives by, and the passion and spirit that drives his success.

Everett Kircher was the only son of very resourceful and disciplined parents. His early years taught him great respect for their hard work and strong values. Growing up during the Depression and witnessing his father's ability to not only survive but flourish, taught Kircher important practical lessons. These lessons would serve him well in his early business ventures – which included building and selling house trailers, an automobile dealership and a defense contract business during World War II.

The Early Years

My maternal great grandfather, whose surname was Ruede, was of Swiss descent. After coming to America, he first settled in Illinois. The Civil War broke out and he joined the Union Army. He was encamped in Missouri when the war ended in 1865. He married a girl of Swiss and French ancestry and they homesteaded and raised a family in a town he named Blooming Rose. It was 150 miles south of St. Louis and he became its first postmaster. He had two sons: my great uncles, Frank and Will, who became two of my favorite relatives. They were the ones who taught me to hunt and fish, pastimes that became important to my life and served as catharsis from the tensions of running my businesses.

My paternal grandfather was a German who immigrated to America and settled in

St. Louis, taking a German girl as his bride. He got a job as a horse-drawn trolley conductor. Their marriage produced a son, John, who would become my father after he married Hilda Louise Metzger.

At the time they were married, my father worked in a rug factory, making $12 a week. His father was the factory foreman. Then my father saw an ad in the St. Louis Post Dispatch placed by the Ford Motor Company in Detroit. Ford was offering $5 a day for factory workers — an unheard of wage back then. People called Ford crazy. Crazy like a fox! To sell his cars he realized that people had to be able to afford them. Paying his workers high wages created a market that hadn't existed.

My father packed a small knapsack and headed to Detroit by train, leaving my mother behind. As soon as he could, he sent for her. Their first home was a tiny house they rented on the east side of Detroit.

I was born in my Grandmother's house in St. Louis on the kitchen table with a midwife assisting. I'm told the midwife cut the umbilical cord with a kitchen knife after she sterilized it on her apron. The date was July 15, 1916. My mother was 19 at the time and my entry into the world was exactly 11 months and three days after my parents were married.

My mother, Hilda Louise Kircher, was one tough lady. Barely over five feet tall and weighing no more than 100 pounds, she was the family disciplinarian and I, being her only child, was the disciplinee. She took "spare the rod and spoil the child" as dogma, and no way was I going to escape unscathed when I misbehaved or got into trouble.

It wasn't until years later, when she was laid up with a broken leg and I took over the cooking, washing and keeping the company books, that I first came to believe that she even liked me, much less loved me.

My father seldom interfered when my mother dished out her brand of punishment. He was the breadwinner. Keeping a kid in line was woman's work. He was over six feet tall and weighed over 200 pounds. He was physically strong, as well as strong-willed, a seemingly tireless worker in his younger days. I didn't inherit his size, but he did pass along his work ethic and many of his beliefs – particularly his ultra-conservative, anti-liberal political convictions.

My father never went beyond the fourth grade but he could read and write very well, which certainly says something about the quality of education our kids are getting today. Many high school and even college graduates can't read or write. I believe it's criminal. Standards have been lowered so much by liberal "feel-good-about-yourself" educators that employers often have to retrain college graduates in basic reading, spelling, grammar and arithmetic before they can handle simple jobs and be productive. American kids are cheated out of a decent education by the philosophy that no child should have his psyche damaged or his self-esteem lowered because he or she happens to have a mite less native intelligence than his or her respective peers.

After laboring a few months on the assembly line, sometimes working seven days a week, my father decided that factory work wasn't the way he wanted to spend his life. He got a job with the Denby Motor Truck Company and learned to be a mechanic. The company went broke, so my father decided to start his own business. He began repairing trucks and cars outdoors, rain or shine. Good mechanics were scarce and having a natural ability for mechanical things, he rapidly built a reputation for good work at a fair price. I remember that he charged $12 to tear down an engine block, grind the valves, and put the block back together. Even at those wages he put enough money aside to buy property on the east side of Detroit, where he intended to build a repair garage. I think he paid $200 for the property, a hefty sum in those days. The lot was in a predominantly Polish neighborhood. Most of the houses and buildings were blue, and the air was usually filled with the smell of cooking cabbage.

One of my earliest childhood recollections was when I was visiting my grandmother in Blooming Rose, Missouri in 1919. I was three years old, sitting on a little three-legged stool that my daughter Kathryn now has; one that has been repaired a hundred times or more. My head was tilted back. Grandmother was holding my nose and spooning castor oil down my throat. That's when I first noticed the gas lights. And I remembered seeing a long gray building with lots of doors. Outhouses! I remember them clearly, probably because I had to visit one a few moments after my grandmother poured castor oil down my throat.

There's not a whole lot I recall of those pre-school years. I was small for my age, so I didn't start kindergarten until I was six. In grade school, I hung around with the neighborhood kids, played sports and managed to stay out of trouble most of the time. Just a normal kid doing kid things.

I had my first personal adventure into the world of entrepreneurs when my father decided to build a garage on the lot he had bought. He made a deal to buy used bricks from a factory building that had been torn down. It was my job to clean the bricks for a penny a brick. After a day or two, I started thinking like Tom Sawyer, and enlisted a few of my neighborhood pals to help, I paid them two cents for three bricks, leaving me a tidy profit. Although most of my later business ventures seldom returned that high a percentage of profit, all were successful, except two: my Chrysler car dealership and my wartime machine shop. I managed to break even on the dealership after selling the showroom and inventory. I just walked away from the machine shop when the war was over. The ancient machines weren't worth anything except as scrap.

My dad built most of the new garage himself, using salvaged materials except for two roof beams and two 12-foot garage doors. I learned a lot from that, too. In my early years when building Boyne Mountain, money was scarce. The first chairlift that got Boyne off and running was second hand (paid $2,000), as was much of the equipment used to clear slopes, groom snow, move earth and build buildings. Fortunately, I had a good grasp of mechanics, thanks to early observations and work in my Dad's garage. Plus, I learned the value of a dollar. That experience has paid off a thousand times over.

My dad worked hard at the truck repair business. Twelve hour days were normal except for Sunday afternoons. That was the time the family would go for a ride in our Chandler automobile. The Fourth of July was always special. We'd mount American flags on the Chandler's radiator cap and tour the city and outskirts. It was a time in our history when everybody was proud to be an American. They were the years before Roosevelt.

Most years we'd take family vacations in the summer to see relatives in St. Louis and Blooming Rose. As a kid I loved those vacations, especially when we'd go to Blooming Rose. That's where I learned to hunt and fish. My Uncle Frank was the hunter. He'd get me up early to go squirrel hunting. I'd hunt with an L.S. Smith double barrel 20 gauge shotgun that Uncle Frank gave me. We didn't go after turkey or deer. Those once abundant populations had been virtually wiped out by early settlers who needed the meat. There were no bag limits or seasons back then, so the deer and turkey disappeared. In recent years both species have come back in strong numbers, thanks to regulated game seasons and bag limits.

We'd always take a dog called Drum along when we went after squirrels. The dog would sniff out the squirrel trails, follow them and tree the game. To be successful, you usually had to have two hunters because the squirrels would always hide on the far side of a tree after they spotted you. After shooting a squirrel or two, it was my job to skin them. My aunt would often make squirrel stew for dinner.

In the evenings after the squirrel hunt, my Uncle Will, Frank's brother, would take me fishing for bass on the nearby Big Piney River. This was my introduction to a sport that I learned to love and will pursue every year as long as I am able.

The family did very well in my early years. Actually my dad made more money during the depression then at any other time in his life. By 1931, he'd saved enough to buy another piece of property, plus enough to build a house. Being busy in the garage, he contracted the house out to a builder for $10,000, and we moved in just as I was finishing the eighth grade, and about to enroll in high school. It was a two-story house with two bedrooms, a bathroom, a kitchen and a living room upstairs. The downstairs was a rental unit. It was rented out first as a fish and chips restaurant, and in the summer the smell of fish competed with the cabbage odor. Later, it was rented out as an auto parts store that my family owned.

I began high school at Northeastern High on Detroit's east side in 1931. We had an ethnic student mix: mostly Polish, some Italians and Irish, and a few African Americans. The school was divided into "houses." Three in all. I was in Angel house. I played softball and football on the Angel team.

I got the leading role in the senior play, "Patsy." It was the story about a guy in love with a girl who brushed him off for another guy. That's where the term "Patsy" comes from. Sometimes, I feel I've played that role in real life.

The country was stalled in the Great Depression all during those high school years. Our family had no financial worries. But many in Detroit and the nation really had to scrimp. Banks closed. There were soup kitchens. No welfare or food stamps. School teachers and city employees were paid in script. Everybody had a vegetable garden. Lots of kids went to CCC camps. But I was one of the lucky ones. I graduated from Northeastern High in 1935 and, at age 19, I got accepted by the University of Michigan. But I remember my high school days and classmates to this day. We have a Northeastern High School class reunion every year at Boyne Mountain, though the classmate ranks are thinning. We held our 61st anniversary in 1996, playing golf, reminiscing and generally having a good time.

After my freshman year at the University of Michigan, the family decided to go to California for a summer vacation – my mother and father, my Aunt Ruby and Ruby's son Freddie, left on the trip. I had talked my father into buying a house trailer. In those days they were strictly trailers purely for towing behind a car. Our trailer was made in Mt. Clemens, Michigan, and was called "The Covered Wagon." It was one of the first trailers ever manufactured. The retail cost was about $450.

On the way to California the family stopped at the side of the road near Rabbit Ear Pass, Colorado. It was raining. The roadside was wet and slippery, and the car and trailer got stuck. My mother, Aunt Ruby and cousin Freddie, who was about 8 at the time, got out of the car and started to push, with my father gunning the engine. In the rush of getting out, the car hit the pavement, lurched ahead with the trailer, knocked my mother down and the trailer ran over her leg, breaking it badly in a number of places.

They rushed her to the nearest town, Steamboat Springs. There was no ski area there yet, and only one doctor. He put her leg in a traction cast, and the family drove home, traveling day and night. I still can't believe that they would do that. She really suffered. It reminded me of the covered wagon days. If you got sick they left you beside the trail or, if you were lucky, at the nearest civilization.

Their trip ended my formal college education, but was the beginning of my real education, learning by doing in the College of Hard Knocks.

I took care of my mother while her leg healed and helped my father in the garage for a while. Then a friend told me about an outfit planning to build a house trailer. It was to have a one-piece rounded top, stamped out on a giant press, and rounded windows, like those of the Studebaker that had caused such a sensation. It was called the Streamlight. All metal. Sixteen feet overall.

I talked my father into investing $5,000 in the trailer business. We formed a partnership. It was a 50-50 deal. I provided the labor, he provided the seed money. The trailer company granted me a franchise, and I used the money to buy product and open a salesroom on Woodward Avenue in Detroit's old Convention Hall.

The business grew to be successful in a hurry. Then another house trailer line became available. It was made in Chicago. As I recall, I paid $375 for the smallest ones, and sold them for $450 apiece. With the profits, I bought more and rented them out at $50 a week. People were hot to rent. I figured that in eight or nine weeks I could pay for a trailer from rental income. By the end of a year, I had a whole fleet of rentals and was going great guns.

Even though my trailer business took off quickly and was doing great, I became stupid, too big for my britches. I took all of the money I had made in trailer sales and took on a Chrysler automobile dealership franchise, an expensive showroom, employees, a repair garage, a large car inventory and plenty of headaches.

Not concentrating on expanding the trailer business and using it as a stepping stone into manufacturing mobile homes was the biggest business mistake I ever made. I could have been in on the ground floor of an industry destined to explode in the late 1940s. Although I would have made a fortune by just manufacturing the small trailers at $450, I could have become a millionaire quickly had I branched out into the infant and highly profitable industry of manufacturing the larger mobile homes.

I didn't abandon the trailer business completely when I took on the auto dealership. I kept selling them from my used car lot. That kept me alive during the hard times in the auto industry. Then, Japan bombed Pearl Harbor and World War II began. I had a lot of car inventory on hand that the government wouldn't let me sell — car sales were frozen for the duration — but I had to pay interest on the inventory. Chrysler was forced to switch from manufacturing cars to making defense equipment. The trailer companies shutdown too, and I was out of business.

Chrysler wanted to maintain their dealership organization, so they offered to sub-contract some of their defense work to those dealers able to set up and convert to job-shop machining of defense parts.

My dealership building was not large enough to house a bunch of machinery, so I moved out and back into my dad's old garage, the one I helped build by chipping bricks. Machinery dealers were dragging out old, obsolete line-shaft equipment discarded years before and selling it at auctions. I bought some ancient lathes and screw machines, most of which weren't even motorized. They were belt-driven. You had to convert them yourself with conversion kits. Detroit became known as the Arsenal of Democracy, and I became a part of it.

I hired some skilled workers and learned how to operate all of the machinery. We began making all kinds of small parts for tanks. Mostly bolts. Branching out from Chrysler's war contracts, I began soliciting work from other government contractors. We got into aircraft studs and threading. That led to building five inch rocket cones. The cones were used on Navy rockets and were tricky to build. They had left-handed threads on the inside and two other internal threads, plus one external thread. They all had to run concentric to each other. Fortunately, my factory was the only shop making this part. It was the biggest war contract I ever had and it was very important to the Navy. They even stationed a Navy lieutenant at the plant to assure that we produced quality cones to very tight tolerances.

At one point during the war, I had as many as 30 employees working three shifts. Did I make much money during these years? The answer is "no." After selling the machinery at war's end, I figured I'd broken even. But I had stayed afloat and gained a lot of mechanical and basic engineering experience that turned out to be invaluable when I got into the ski business.

Most business ventures start small, and Boyne is no exception. In the late 1940s, Kircher and two friends thought that Michigan should have its own major ski resort and began the search. Here, he relays the story of the birth of Boyne Ski Lodge, Inc. – the people involved, how the site was selected and how the land was attained. Every good idea starts with a dream.

Boyne Mountain circa 1950

Search for a Michigan Mountain

"Wouldn't it be great if Michigan had a real ski mountain?" This rhetorical question always popped up whenever Michigan skiers got together. Back then, in the 1940s, most of us who wanted a mountain experience had to go to Stowe, Vermont, Mt. Tremblant in Canada, or out to Sun Valley. Aspen was just getting started and Vail hadn't even been thought of.

Going to Sun Valley in those days was a three-day trip by train, or five days by car. We didn't have expressways, so Stowe and Tremblant weren't all that close, either.

One weekend I was sitting around the lodge at the Otsego Ski Club in Gaylord, Michigan, talking to the Booth family about how great it would be if we had a real mountain in Michigan. Like other early ski areas in the state, Otsego's 250 feet vertical was about tops. The Booths, who were cross-country skiers as well as downhillers, had recently climbed a pretty high peak near Lake Louise, about 25 miles north.

After checking it out, I got pretty excited about the possibilities but the euphoria didn't last long. The property was owned by the Methodist Church which frowned on alcoholic beverages. I couldn't envision a ski area where booze was outlawed.

Later that winter I met with two ski buddies, John Norton and Jim Christianson. Norton was a civil engineer and Christianson was an executive with the Detroit Boy Scout Council. We had skied together at Otsego, Sun Valley and other areas. We all wanted more skiing challenges. It was then that we decided to get serious about finding a mountain-like slope in Michigan, if indeed there was one.

Norton got the ball rolling. He secured some topographical maps from the state conservation department. Studying them, we determined that the most promising spot to begin hunting was northwest Michigan in the lower peninsula. We pinpointed ten different locations with elevations of a thousand feet or more, most being within 50 miles of the town of Gaylord. There were higher peaks in the upper peninsula, but we figured they would be too far north for travelers from Detroit.

We operated out of a hunting cabin I owned on the Manistee river. Over long weekends that summer we inspected all ten sites. We ran topos of the slopes, checked altitudes, exposures and other things that we thought would affect skiing conditions. We also wanted easy highway accessibility. The sixth site turned out to be our final choice after inspecting all ten. It was the highest peak on a ridge just outside the crossroads town of Boyne Falls, about seven miles east of Boyne City and 17 miles south of the summer resort city of Petoskey. The elevation was over 1,150 feet with a vertical slightly more than 500 feet, about double that of other ski areas in the state.

Providing we could buy or lease the property, we would clear the main run facing northeast, meaning it would hold snow longer, well into spring. Also, the site lay in the region of the greatest snowfall in the central United States, averaging over 10 feet annually. And because of the proximity of Lake Michigan 25 miles away, we could expect "lake effect" snow: moisture-laden winds off the lake funneled down a gap formed by Lake Charlevoix. These prevailing northwesterlies sweep upward when hitting our mountain range. This drastic change in altitude and temperature causes abnormal precipitation, resulting in heavy quantities of snow, year in and year out.

After settling on the site, our next step was to try and buy it. A man named William Pierson of Boyne City, a former legislator and a fine gentleman, owned the property we wanted. John, Jim and I each anted up $5,000 seed money we thought would be needed to buy the property. When we told Pierson why we wanted it, he said, "Anybody damn fool enough to want to build a ski hill, well ... I'll give you the property." So we had an attorney draw up the papers and we bought Pierson's 40 acres for $1.00, which included the land where the main lodge now stands.

In the spring of 1947, the three of us formed Boyne Ski Lodge, Inc. I became president, John, vice president, and Jim, treasurer.

As soon as we locked up the property we decided to get started. But we felt we needed more land at the base of our property line to locate the lodge we planned to build. That would give us a few more feet of vertical and a longer runout.

This parcel was owned by a family named Skop, who lived in Detroit and worked at the Dodge Brothers auto plant. The family signed a lease with an option for us to buy. When it came time to exercise our option with the Skops, they refused to sell. They were downright belligerent and nasty about it. I finally had to hire an attorney to talk to them and they still refused. After taking the case to court, we figured it would take a couple of years to get a suit resolved and decided to go ahead and build the lodge on the spot where it's located now.

I'm still not happy about it. Had we been able to build the lodge on the Skop parcel, we would have been able to cluster our main buildings closer together and have longer runouts on all of our slopes. I vowed at the time that if I ever started another ski area I'd lock up all the land needed before a single tree was cut.

Often when we are young we discover something that sparks a fire inside of us. Some of us pursue it as a hobby, some keep it as a dream, others ignore it altogether – and a few dedicate their lives to it. For Kircher, this spark was alpine skiing, and not only did it change his life, but all of ours, too.

Love of Skiing

I've always liked all the seasons of the year. That's why I chose to live in northern Michigan. But I fell in love with a snowflake, and winter became my favorite season, and skiing my favorite sport.

I was 20 before I bought my first pair of skies. They were the Northland brand, sold by J.L. Hudson Co., Detroit's major department store. They were wooden, and over seven feet long with beartrap bindings. The edges were wooden, too, so Hudson's routed out side grooves and installed metal edges that screwed on and needed constant maintenance and blocking to retain their camber. I tried them out a few times on slopes and other hills around Detroit, but kept crossing the tails.

I took those skis on my first real ski trip. It was to Lake Placid, site of the 1932 Winter Olympics. I kept crossing the tails. The "expert" at the ski shop told me the problem was that the skis were too long for a guy my size. He fixed them by cutting about two inches off of the tips. Not surprisingly, this ski surgery didn't work.

I then bought a pair of hickory skis made by Stein Eriksen's father in Norway. They were wider than normal and had very soft tips, ideal for skiing in deep snow. Looking back, I think that these were the best skis I ever owned for deep snow, perfect for the powder that the western mountains offer skiers.

The next year, l938, I went to Sun Valley which had opened the year before. I found out about Sun Valley by attending a travel show at the Detroit City Convention Hall. They were offering a ski week package, including rail transportation, skiing, lodging and food for $150. It was the first ski package I had ever discovered and at that price, I jumped at it.

Hans Hauser was Sun Valley's director of skiing and he'd recruited a bunch of Europeans to teach the sport. Victor Gottchaulk was my first instructor. Later, he came to work for me at Boyne Mountain as ski school director, and we named the Victor Run after him.

Everybody was teaching the Arlberg technique back then. It had been developed by Hannes Schneider, and Hans Hauser had brought it to Sun Valley. Hauser had been a student of Professor Stefan Krukenhauser, Austria's State Director of Ski Instructors. The technique was rotation-based. You'd plant a pole, unweigh your skis by a sudden upwards movement of your body, turn your shoulders and hips in the direction you wanted to go, and the skis would follow along. You could make nice round turns using the Arlberg method, but it wasn't very efficient for slalom racing. You couldn't run a flush very quickly. Your hip would fly out, you'd lose your edges and overturn. But that was the system being taught all over the world, and the way I learned.

I went to Sun Valley for 13 consecutive years on my annual vacation. It was a glamorous place, with all sorts of celebrities and movie stars. It was the place to go in the winter for the rich and famous. You'd see people like Gary Cooper, Clark Gable, Claudette Colbert, Ann Southern, Ingrid Bergman, Jimmy Stewart and many others. John Payne played there in Glenn Miller's band before he became a movie star and got the male lead with Sonja Henie in the movie Sun Valley Serenade. Nelson Rockefeller would visit regularly, arriving in his private railway car, bringing an entourage of friends and relatives.

I drank in Sun Valley and all its sights, sounds and glamour like a thirsty camel, storing away much of it in my mind. I was intrigued by the outdoor swimming pools at the Lodge and Challenger Inn. Seeing skiers frolic in the heated pools in the winter with the snow coming down made an indelible impression on me, and I later copied the idea for Boyne resorts along with other things I had observed at Sun Valley. (I've never been bashful about borrowing an idea from anyone as long as it was a sound one. I'm not one who needs to reinvent the wheel — just improve it whenever possible.)

I couldn't take as much time from work as I'd like for trips out West, so on winter weekends I'd try to ski somewhere. There were some decent slopes just outside of Detroit, and at Detroit Metro Riverside Park, owned by the city. It had ice rinks and a number of toboggan runs. No ski tows, of course. So I built my own, copied from a Swedish rope tow I'd seen.

Being in the machine business, I was able to build my own wheels. I bought a long length of rope, spliced the ends, and mounted a Briggs-Stratton engine on a toboggan. Friends and I would load the apparatus in the trunk of my car along with a couple of batteries and some sealed-beam headlights. We'd put the lights up and run the rope assembly down, hooking onto a tree below. Then we'd pull the toboggan by car to tighten up the rope, start up the Briggs-Stratton and away we'd go. I can't count how many times I used that old rope tow. Even used it at Boyne Mountain down the backside of the ridge. It was on display in the lodge lobby for a number of years and is now gathering rust somewhere in one of our storage garages.

The more I skied, the more interested I became in technique. Whenever I spotted a good skier I'd talk with him, asking how he made a particular turn or other maneuver. I was out at Sun Valley one season, skiing with Marty Arrouge. He was a Basque, married to movie star Norma Shearer, and had been a ski school instructor at the Valley. Marty had been to the 1952 Winter Olympics, watching the ski races. He was trying to show me how the young racers were skiing. A new, counter-rotation method. He kept flopping around and falling down, even though he was an excellent Arlberg skier. The technique didn't have a name. Some called it the reverse shoulder. Later it had various names: wedlyn, short swing and mombo are three names I recall.

I was determined to find out more about this method, both for myself and for Boyne Mountain skiers, so I recruited Norwegian Stein Eriksen to direct the ski school at Boyne Mountain. Eriksen had used this reverse shoulder style to win a gold medal in the giant slalom in the '52 Olympics and the triple gold – the slalom, giant slalom and downhill in the '54 Federation International de Ski Championships (FIS).

Don Thomas, an employee of mine at my car dealership and a member of Boyne's ski patrol on weekends, had seen Eriksen ski at the '52 games. When Eriksen visited America to train at Sun Valley, Don sold him a Studebaker. We were introduced and I suggested he think about coming to Boyne, but he wanted to compete in the '54 FIS first. After his triple win, we began communicating regularly. He finally agreed to come for $5,000, an amount to this day he insists was $10,000.

Eriksen came to the Mountain for the '55 season, bringing a number of his Norwegian skier buddies with him. He was blonde, handsome and the most beautiful skier you'd ever seen, gliding over the snow like a bird sailing on the wind. People would stop and watch, and everybody wanted to ski like him. His ski school classes were packed and his private lesson book was constantly filled. His reverse shoulder style wasn't easy to explain or teach, however. He had learned it by doing; finding a faster way to make tight turns in slalom races. No step-by-step method of instruction had been perfected. Even our other instructors had a difficult time getting it to a point where they could demonstrate the turn, much less teach it.

The young kids learned it more quickly than the older skiers. They mimicked and picked it up easily. By the end of the season, I got the hang of it, but couldn't describe any certain way to make the switch from Arlberg to reverse shoulder.

Eriksen stayed for three ski seasons. When he left, I asked him, "Who can I get to teach this new thing?" He said, "Othmar Schneider." Eriksen knew Schneider well, having competed with him in the Olympics.

Schneider, an Austrian, had been a student of the Krukenhauser school, the official ski instruction school of Austria, and was a superb technician as well as a fantastic ski racer. He was an Austrian national hero, not only for ski racing but as an Olympic champion in pistol shooting.

With the 1956 ski season approaching, I was anxious to get Schneider to head our ski school. He wasn't answering my letters. Chuck Moll and I decided that the only way we'd get him was for one of us to go to Portillo, Chile, where Schneider was director of their ski school during our off season summer months.

Chuck was elected. He flew to Washington, D.C., and pulled off a major miracle by getting a passport overnight, thanks to Congressman Gerald Ford. (While still in Congress, Mr. Ford and his family were frequent visitors to Boyne Mountain). Chuck flew to Portillo and got Schneider to agree to become Boyne's director of skiing.

Schneider came to Boyne and headed up the ski school for 17 years. He hand-picked and brought along other Krukenhauser graduates, young guys and girls who had gone through the four-year Krukenhauser course, earned ski instructor degrees and were proficient in teaching the modern ski technique.

To get these talented Austrians over here on a visa, we had an annual fight with the Immigration Department. We insisted that there weren't any ski instructors in the United States qualified to teach the new method. One had to be a certified Krukenhauser graduate to teach the new, revolutionary technique, we claimed. That was the only way we could secure visas for the Austrians, so they could instruct for the entire season.

Schneider ruled the ski school with an iron fist, like a Prussian general training troops and leading them into battle. Under him the Boyne Ski School became the envy of the industry. We were really at the forefront of the new technique for quite a long time. I know this because Schneider would take trips to Aspen and Sun Valley, and found that their ski schools were still teaching the Arlberg method.

Many instructors who taught at Boyne were lured away to other resorts to head up ski schools, a fact that I often resented but couldn't avoid. In more recent years, a number of major ski areas began teaching the "wide track". It is nothing more than a dipsy doodle. It's not related to the movements we use in the modern technique. It's a series of short snow-plow turns, often with a stem. Your feet are apart, like the racers. It looks ugly and we don't allow our ski schools to teach it.

From the first time I strapped those long wooden boards on my feet, I fell in love with skiing. I'm proud to have been able to help contribute to the growth of this graceful, invigorating sport.

Stein Erikson gained world wide recognition as an Olympic Gold Medal winner. Having met Everett Kircher early in the 1950s, he bought a car from Kircher and later agreed to become the head of Boyne's ski school. Stein became an admirer of Kircher's and a life long friend.

Through other eyes

Stein Eriksen

I first met Everett Kircher on my way back to Norway from Sun Valley where I had been training for the 1952 Olympics. I bought a new Studebaker automobile from his Detroit dealership. Kircher and I talked, and he asked me if I would be interested in coming to his ski resort in Michigan to head up his ski school. I told him I'd think about it, but the 1954 FIS world championships had to come first.

After the competitions and contacts from Boyne, I accepted Everett's offer. My amateur days were over, and Kircher's was the first firm offer that I'd had. I thought that starting in a little ski area would be the best way for me to accumulate a little experience and see how it worked out. (To this day I claim that he paid me $10,000 for that first year. He says it was only $5,000. Now, 40 years later, we still kid each other about who's right and who's wrong. Regardless, it was a satisfying arrangement for both of us and one that I will never regret.)

When I arrived at Boyne for the '54-55 ski season as director of the ski school, I was amazed to find 400 to 500 people in Boyne's weekly learn-to-ski weeks. That was an incredible accomplishment for any ski resort back then.

My gold medals in the Olympics and world championships had brought my reverse shoulder racing technique to Everett's attention. He was insistent that my instructors teach it exclusively, being convinced that it was the technique of the future for racers and for recreational skiers, and that it would replace the Arlberg rotation method being taught at most ski resorts around the world.

I headed up the Boyne Mountain ski school for three years, and developed a great admiration for the man. He had an incredible ingenuity about what the skiing public needed and wanted and what the business required. If the learn-to-ski-weekers didn't know what skiing was all about when they came to Boyne, they did by the time they left.

Everett was years ahead of everyone when it came to developing and operating a ski resort and attracting the potential skiing public. I don't think the industry realizes what an important part he has played in the development of Alpine skiing in the United States. I think that when people learn more about what Everett has contributed to skiing, he will be remembered as one of the dedicated pioneers of the business.

Everett Kircher should be in every ski hall of fame for what he did for the ski industry in its infancy.

Boyne Mountain ski lodge - 1955.

Kircher's garage in downtown Detroit.

Mr. and Mrs. Kircher, Everett's mother and father.

Kircher and his favorite sport.

A lone skier in the early days of Boyne Mountain stands
at the top of Hemlock.

Boyne Mountain, Circa 1949.

Boyne Mountain
when trails were not
as numerous.

Early ski lodge facilities at Boyne.

Today's snow making effort.

Othmar Schneider, 1961.

Boyne Mountain expanded dramatically in the 1960s.

Snow guns roar day and night at Boyne facilities
ensuring good conditions throughout winter.

Everett's mother and father at a Boyne function.

Everett and his son John Kircher.

Gerald Ford was a regular at Boyne in the early years.

Stein Eriksen in the mid 1950s.

The leader board at an initial ski competition, 1961.

NO.	NAME		TIME		NO.
1	LEITNER	47.31	47.05	94.36	1
2	HINTERSEER	47.40	47.83	95.23	2
3	GRAMSHAMMER	48.24	47.23	95.47	3
4	ZIMMERMAN	47.88	47.91	95.79	4
5	BONLIEU	48.09	47.97	96.27	5
6	PRAVDA	48.85	47.51	96.36	6
7	ERIKSEN	48.25	48.46	96.71	7
8	SCHNEIDER	48.13	48.92	97.05	8
9	HOFSENBERGER	48.95	48.93	97.88	9
10	QUEHENBERGER	49.24	48.85	98.09	10
11	GASPERL	51.01	49.75	100.76	11
12	VAUGHN	54.87	49.89	104.76	12
13	TRAUNER	1.01.81	49.60	151.41	13
14	SCHWARZ	49.70	1.02.17	151.87	14
	MOLTERER	46.89	DNF		15
	DUVILLARD	DISQ	47.35		16
	STAUB	DISQ	47.26		17

The early days of Boyne Ski Lodge Inc. were very exciting. Kircher and crew decided that if a ski resort in Michigan was going to work, it had to start with a bang! Therefore, they cleared some of the biggest runs in the state, built one of the grandest lodges and installed the first chairlift in the Midwest. Here, Kircher relays not only how Boyne got that lift - but the story of the historical lift itself.

Boyne Mountain circa 1950

The First Chairlift

Norton, Christianson and I had started Boyne Mountain as a lark. A fun thing where we could have some challenging skiing without going out West or to the East. We never dreamed of it as a potential business venture, much less a vocation for any of us.

Foremost on our minds was that next to snow, the most important thing in downhill skiing was getting uphill. The easier and faster the better. Transportation was the name of the game.

So when planning our rope tow system, Victor Gottschalk mentioned that Sun Valley was making some changes and might have a used chairlift for sale that we could get cheap.

Victor had been my ski instructor at Sun Valley for eight years. He was a colorful guy and a superb skier. He had started skiing at age four in his native Garmish, in southern Germany. He had skied and taught the sport all over Europe; Kreuzeck, Mittenwalk, Zell an See, St. Moritz, Pontresina, Piz Palii, as well as Kiska and Attu in Alaska. He came to Idaho on a hunting trip, and ran into old buddy Hans Hauser, who was recruiting a corps of European instructors for Sun Valley's initial opening.

I had hired Victor to help me lay out our original runs, promising him the job of head instructor when Boyne opened. We scratched out the runs in ink over glossy aerial photographs. When Victor told me about the Sun Valley lift, I didn't waste a minute. I made an offer of $2,000, got verbal acceptance, followed up with a contract, and the deal was done.

We bought the chairlift, lock, stock and broken wires. It was the first chairlift ever built in the world. The single-person chairs had worn, leather-padded seats. The towers were wooden utility poles, the cross-arms were also wooden. The cable wheels were in bad shape, but repairable. The bullwheels and upper and lower terminal assemblies were in good condition, needing little repair.

When Victor went out to Sun Valley to tear down the lift, he was the first person to ever dismantle a chairlift. He salvaged everything. The lift, telephone poles, bolts and terminals, and all arrived at the base of Boyne Mountain on flatbed railroad cars early in the summer of 1947.

In addition to his other talents, John Norton was a surveyor. We sat down and made a profile of the mountain. He sighted the line. We poured concrete footings and duplicated hold-downs and hold-ups just as the Sun Valley engineers had done. We followed their measurements exactly, except we kept the distance from the chairs to the ground lower, both having had the unpleasant experience of hanging high above a ski slope, with no safe way off during a stoppage except by ladder.

Buying the Sun Valley chairlift was a decision I'll never regret. It was the first chairlift in the Midwest, and overnight it catapulted Boyne Mountain into the headlines as the top ski area in the Midwest.

History buffs may know the story of that first Sun Valley chairlift, and how it came about. But it bears retelling.

Averill Harriman, chairman of the Union Pacific Railroad, envisioned an exclusive winter resort designed to attract well-heeled visitors from around the world. He commissioned an Austrian nobleman to find a place that would be accessible only by the Union Pacific, be of sufficient distance from large cities so as not to attract hordes of weekend skiers, have mountainous terrain of a variety that would attract skiers of all abilities, have abundant winter snow and months of winter sunshine. The nobleman assigned the search was Count Felix Von Schaffgotsch of Austria. Meeting Harriman's mandates weren't simple. He combed the mountains of Wyoming, Utah, California and Colorado, finally recommending a site he thought to be ideal in the Sawtooth Mountains of Idaho, just outside of the town of Ketchum.

Once a thriving silver mining center, Ketchum was slowly deteriorating. The price of silver had dropped and mining the metal became hardly more than a subsistence endeavor. Most of the miners had left, and many of the businesses along with them. Fortunately, Ketchum was located at the end of a Union Pacific line with no competitive lines anywhere near, nor was there any likelihood that there ever would be. The location met all of Harriman's requirements. Union Pacific bought a 4,300 acre ranch just outside Ketchum and development began.

An early step was the need to promote the developing resort, so Harriman called in PR whiz Steve Hannigan. Hannigan was the guy who put Miami on the map by hyping winter sunshine and a balmy climate. Hannigan used the same strategy, portraying the new ski resort as a place where one could ski in shirt sleeves, and he named it Sun Valley.

The count recommended that the new area needed a cable car for hauling skiers up the mountain, similar to those which a few ski areas in Europe used. Union Pacific wasn't about to shell out that kind of money in the wilderness. And at that time there wasn't anything yet invented that would meet Harriman's demand for swiftly and comfortably moving skiers uphill. In America, there was Fred Pabst's J-bar at Bromley. Yosemite National Park had a 20 person toboggan and most other areas here and abroad had rope tows.

Harriman wanted something different, something better, and not cost prohibitive. From headquarters in Chicago, the Union Pacific engineering staff was assigned the task of inventing a mechanical devise for transporting volume numbers of skiers uphill.

With nothing to go by and no ideas on the horizon, the buck was passed down to James Curren, a self-made bridge engineer who had learned his profession by observing and doing. Much like me, he was product of the hard-knocks school of engineering. He eventually became one of the few engineers to pass a tough state engineering exam without having a college education.

Curren had been employed by Paxton and Verling Iron Works of Omaha, a company that manufactured equipment for loading bananas on boats, using hooks strung on a continuously moving cable. He visualized a device using "hooks" carrying single-person chairs. He submitted drawings of his hook system to his superiors, but it was rejected as too dangerous. Other Union Pacific staff engineers submitted ideas. The brass at Chicago headquarters were antsy to get going and sent word to the engineering department to submit all ideas. Curren slipped his plans into the pile of drawings. It was accepted over all of the others, and the engineering department got the word that the "mono tram"as visualized by

Curren, was to be developed on a priority basis.

At the time, all that the engineering staff knew about snow was how to remove it from railroad tracks – now the brass "wanted to play in the stuff." So in the summer of 1936, the engineers began building two chairlifts from Curren's plans, one for Dollar Mountain, the other for Proctor Mountain. Before the lifts were finalized, a skier named John Morgan was sent to Omaha to solve a major problem. It was imperative to find the maximum speed that the chairs could be loaded safely without stops and starts.

A single chair was rigged to the side of an old pickup truck. Morgan stood on a bed of straw with his skis, and the truck would approach slowly to scoop him up. You can imagine the nose dives he must have taken. The straw was swept away and Morgan donned roller skates instead of skis. The truck's speed was gradually increased until it reached 300 feet per minute, with Morgan able to mount and dismount easily. Thus 300 feet was established as the line speed of the cables for the two lifts.

The revolutionary chairlifts were completed and installed in time for the 1937 winter season. The first passengers were a group of women who volunteered to take the initial historic ride. Enter Murphy's Law: On the very first run on Proctor Mountain, a fuse blew and the ladies were stranded, dangling from the chairs.

It was the same when Boyne Mountain opened 11 years later. Everything was going smoothly as the first riders moved up the Mountain on that identical Dollar Mountain lift. But one of our people had forgotten to refill the gear box with oil. The chairs came to a grinding halt, with the press and onlookers all on hand to witness and report the mishap. The thoughts that crossed my mind at that moment are unprintable. Suffice to say that the wife of the guy who forgot the oil would have become an instant widow if he had been within reach.

I dispatched an employee from my car dealership in Detroit to St. Louis, where a new gear box was available. Then I got a call from him the next day. "Boss, this here gearbox weighs three tons and the pickup is only a half-ton." I told him to improvise, "Jam some two-by-fours between the springs and axle and get your fanny back here as fast as you can." We were back in operation within a week. Boyne Mountain was off and running with the only chairlift in the Midwest.

During the installation of the used lift, we had scrambled to build the lodge and cut in the first two runs on the heavily wooded terrain. The major run – the steepest and longest – we named Hemlock, because of a large, imposing Hemlock tree we intended to save from the woodcutters ax. This run ran from top to bottom, at an average 45-degree pitch. It was the longest and steepest ski run in the Midwest, a challenge to the braver, better skiers.

The tree quickly became a famous landmark. Then one day in the sixties it was cut down by two kids whose parents usually skied at the Otsego Ski Club in Gaylord.

After discovering who the culprits were, I contacted their parents. I told the parents that I wouldn't prosecute their sons if they would each donate $500 to the Republican National Committee. The Republican family agreed, and made the donation. The Democratic family refused. I should have known. It merely reinforced my low opinion of Democrats.

The second run was named Pierson, after the man who had given us the original 40 acres. It took off from about halfway up Hemlock, and circled back to the bottom through the woods. It was quite gentle, perfect for the beginners. They could access the run by riding the chairlift to a halfway station, getting off while the chair continued its journey to the top.

Clearing the runs took a lot of time and labor. We didn't have bulldozers then. We used handsaws to cut down the large, second-growth trees, leaving short stumps. Teams of horses dragged the trees downhill, and we sold the logs to a local lumber yard.

Getting rid of the stumps was another matter. We'd dig a hole under the stump, insert a stick of dynamite, and let 'er blow. The problem with blowing them was that the dynamite just exploded the top of the stump. Jagged roots remained, and they had to be axed out by hand.

We don't clear slopes that way anymore. We use power winches to pull out the whole tree, roots and all. Then we burn the trunks, limbs, roots, and stumps in one big pile. You need the whole log if you're going to burn the stump. On the more gentle slopes, we use bulldozers to get rid of the trees.

Building the original lodge wasn't nearly as eventful as clearing slopes or erecting the chairlift. Among his many talents, John Norton was an architect, as well as a civil engineer, and he designed the lodge and supervised its construction. It was two stories, 40 x 70 feet overall. The lower floor housed a bar we named the Trophy Room, destined to become the site of many memorable apres' ski parties; a place where boy meets girl, boy dates girl, then, boy marries girl. Their grandchildren are now Boyne skiers.

The lower floor also featured restrooms, a cafeteria and a massive Onaway limestone fireplace. The architecture was Swiss Chalet, a motif that we followed as we increased the size of the lodge and added the Boyne Mountain buildings. Some of the lumber we used was milled from the trees we salvaged from clearing the slopes.

Although this section of Michigan was once the headquarters of the lumber industry, we were unable to find timbers large enough to support the roof. We had to import beams to complete the construction, but got the lodge finished in time to open for the 1948 Christmas season.

Many state and local dignitaries, celebrities and press attended our opening.

Don McLouth, president of McLouth Steel and founder of the Otsego Ski Club, was there. One of our Boyne Mountain ski runs is named in his honor. A group of ski professionals were on hand and staged a race for spectators. We also had a good representation from Detroit, Chicago, Grand Rapids and Toledo newspapers, local and national media, and freelance writers.

An old press release that I dug out of the archives reminded me that officials from many organizations were invited and attended. A state senator, a member of the state House of Representatives, Chamber of Commerce officials, folks in the tourist business and others too numerous to list, helped make that day one I'll always remember. For the first time I got the feeling that a ski business in Michigan really did have a future, and me along with it.

An avid skier, Don first met Everett at Boyne Mountain in 1949. Soon after, he went to work for Everett at the car dealership in Detroit. Don has been close to Everett ever since, and has participated in many of Boyne USA's activities and contributed to its growth.

Through other eyes

Don Thomas

In the spring of 1949 I had been skiing at Caberfae, one of Michigan's earliest ski areas. I was working on the ski patrol there to get free skiing, and one weekend that year I went to Boyne Mountain. They had a much better ski mountain and a chairlift, so when I heard that they needed more patrolmen, I signed on.

Owner Everett Kircher was a real taskmaster for the ski patrol. Whenever we had a snowfall we spent half of our day packing snow by foot. Before the patrol was allowed to do any free skiing, the slopes had to be packed for the customers. He also had us do a lot of other work — shoveling walks, packing trails, splicing rope tows, picking up trash, all sorts of maintenance. It was all for the good of the resort and we didn't mind doing it.

After that first year Everett offered me a job as a salesman for his Studebaker dealership in Detroit. One of my sales was to Stein Eriksen whom I had met in Europe at the Winter Olympics.

Everett bounced back and forth between the car dealership and the Mountain, overseeing both operations. From the beginning he was a hands-on guy. The single-place chairlifts he had bought from Sun Valley were converted to doubles at the dealership with Everett working as hard as anybody.

Another ski project we undertook at the car dealership was building a snow packer that the boss had designed. It consisted of bicycle wheels and wooden slats, his first attempt at a mechanical packer. I was in charge of that project, but it was only moderately successful — too light to do the job well. But it was the forerunner of modern packers that Boyne developed through the years.

I skied Boyne on weekends, and Everett and I became very good friends. While there, I proposed to a gal named Edna that I had met while skiing. Luckily for me, she accepted. We planned on spending our honeymoon in Gatlinburg, Tennessee, at about the same time Everett was considering building a scenic chairlift there. He asked me what I thought of the town and if a chairlift would be a good idea. Having done a bit of research on Gatlinburg, I told him I thought it would be a great place. Millions of people would be going through there to visit the Great Smokey National Park. A scenic lift would be a sure-fire attraction.

Everett and his father, John, built the lift in 1953 and it was a winner right from the start, providing much of the cash flow needed in those early years to develop Boyne Mountain. "It's an oil well, a gusher," he told me. And it's been flowing ever since.

In 1953, I quit my auto salesman's job and started a successful retail ski sales business. Our friendship continued to grow. Quite often we'd go with our wives to his hunting and fishing cabin on the Manistee River. I wasn't much of a fisherman, but Everett was a nut about fly fishing for trout. I'd paddle my little heart out while he fished. "Back water, back water, go forward, go forward, on the right, on the left." He wanted to be in just the right place to cast his fly where he thought a fish was lurking. He was the captain of the ship and I was the crew. But I enjoyed it. It was a lot of fun being around Everett and still is.

On week-nights we'd often ski around Detroit. Everett had designed and built this little rope tow and equipped it with automobile headlights. He powered it with a small gasoline engine that was powerful enough to get the job done. We'd go to Riverbank Park or

Teeple Hill, hook it up to a tree and do our thing. That rope tow is an example of Everett's ingenuity. He was always farsighted, a visionary, an inventor, and is to this day.

Everett was always positive. Whatever the project was, he never accepted the thought that it couldn't be done. He never took no for an answer. "It can be done, we can do it. Let's just do it. Let's get it done." That kind of thinking and determination led to the double chairlifts, the triple and four-place chairs, and to many developments in snowmaking and snow conditioning that revolutionized skiing and are in use today around the world.

One day Everett Kircher will be recognized and credited for all he has done for the ski business, and for how he has spearheaded the golf business in northern Michigan. To me, and to his many close friends, he'll always be a fun guy, a regular guy, a wonderful friend and buddy. My life has been enriched knowing him.

Kircher's reputation as an early pioneer in building ski-lifts resulted in an interest in a chairlift in Gatlinburg, Tennessee. Rather than build the lift for Gatlinburg business interests, Kircher invested in Gatlinburg property and built the lift as part of his rapidly expanding Boyne enterprises. The Gatlinburg lift has been an important revenue source since its inception, helping to support other Boyne ventures.

Gatlinburg Lift

One winter day in 1953, I got a call from Gatlinburg, Tennessee. It was from a local innkeeper named Rel Maples. He had read about Boyne and its chairlift in AAA Magazine.

"I want you to build me a scenic chairlift," he said. I told him I was interested, but I wouldn't build it for him, I'd build it for myself if a lift there seemed to have good potential, and if I could lease or buy the right property.

Gatlinburg is located in a narrow valley at the foot of the Great Smoky Mountain National Park. It was, and still is, a funnel for folks driving from coast to coast, and for hordes of vacationing tourists from everywhere.

I set up a date to meet with Mr. Maples and drove to Gatlinburg. That part of the country is very interesting. From an airplane you can see the difference in the way land was once divided to the way it's now done.

The early settlers staked out their lands by a system called *metes and bounds*, a method to define property lines. They'd spot a tree here, a boulder there, maybe a river. They used almost any identifiable object to establish the perimeters of property they bought or homesteaded. The terrain looks like Europe's from the air. Zigzag lines. No squares or rectangles. No rhyme or reason to the parcels. It reminds you of a jigsaw puzzle.

Maples had a small hotel called the Gatlinburg Inn at the center of town. Right behind it on his property was a mountain with a steep vertical rise. There wasn't a road going up there, hardly even a path. And installing a lift on those steep and rocky slopes wouldn't be a piece of cake. But the potential for business looked good.

Maples wouldn't sell me any of his property. Townsfolk didn't sell property down there. A few of the town's original families owned most of the land. But Maples agreed to a 99-year lease on a 30-foot easement. I agreed to pay him out of lift revenues on a graduated scale to a top of 15%. It was all I thought I could afford. I had the papers drawn up and we made the deal.

Nobody was manufacturing chairlifts about that time. I couldn't have afforded a new one anyway. The budget I'd established for the whole project was $10,000. But I had gotten wind of a used lift that was for sale by the Sugar Bowl ski area in California for about $3,000. I decided to buy it, but had to bear the expense of tearing it down.

Vic Chmielewski, head of Boyne's maintenance crew, went to California and dismantled the lift. He had it shipped to Rochester, Michigan, where my father had moved his Studebaker dealership to be near a cabin he was converting for future retirement.

Back in Detroit, at my dealership, I drew up the engineering plans. We kept Snow

Bowl's original chairs, bullwheels and terminal apparatus but had to machine new wheels and make new balance assemblies, which we did in my dealership with some outside machining help.

In February, my father went down to Gatlinburg to scout the place and line up some labor. I joined him a little later after we closed down the ski business for the season.

The first thing we did was hire a surveyor to tell us where the property easement lines were. We tied a flag up in a tree and sighted up from that point to establish our lift line. The route seemed perfect, starting from the main street of town, running alongside Maple's inn, over a river and up this steep, imposing mountain. Before we could start clearing the slope, however, we needed a road to get to the top from the valley floor.

A local and his family lived up near the top of the mountain. If he'd let us cut the road through his property, we told him he could have all the logs. He was delighted. He'd sell the logs, and finally have a way to get down to the town and back without walking.

The mountain had a 1,200-foot vertical drop. I called it Crockett Mountain, after Davy Crockett, the famous woodsman who had roamed and hunted these Tennessee hills for many years.

Pouring the footings for the towers wasn't a snap on that steep, rocky slope. To get water to mix the cement, we had to improvise. We trucked water to the top, then fed it down from station to station through a series of 55 gallon drums connected by garden hoses.

The workers all wanted to know how the chairs sat on the cable. They couldn't imagine a chair dangling from it. We were called crazy Yankees.

The lift was an immediate success. By the third season of operation, we were riding over 100,000 tourists annually. It was the first chairlift ever built in Dixieland, and from the top, tourists have a great view of the town, the valley and the neighboring mountains.

For convenience and for a little extra revenue, we put a gift shop up on top, some snack foods, souvenirs and pay-per-view telescopes. Incidentally, Mr. Maples got his full 15% right from the start.

Boyne Mountain would not have been developed nearly as quickly without this added income from Gatlinburg. Who would have ever guessed that a chairlift in Tennessee would have been one of the main catalysts for the success of Boyne USA?

*In addition to skiing, Kircher discovered another sport early in his life that consumed him –
fishing. In fact, it was this sport, and not skiing, that originally brought him to northern
Michigan. A very decorated angler, Kircher has fished rivers, lakes and oceans around the
world. He has worked extensively to bring these experiences home by significantly contributing
to the raising of Atlantic salmon in northern Michigan rivers and Lake Michigan.*

Hooked on Fishing

As much as I love all types of fishing, going after the Atlantic salmon with a fly rod is

my idea of the ultimate. There's nothing that gets my heart racing more than hooking a big

Atlantic on light tackle and seeing which one of us is going to be the victor. It's often

the fish. But I don't care. There'll be another time, another battle. And if I win, I usually

release him anyway.

I first got hooked on fishing when on vacation in Blooming Rose, Missouri. I was about

12 years old at the time. My great Uncle, Will, took me to the Old Piney River, just out-

side of the town that my great grandfather had founded after his discharge from the Union

Army. I don't remember exactly what kind of fish we were after, or what bait we were using, but I know we caught fish.

From then on, whenever I got the chance, I fished. I don't think there's ever been a year since that first one when I didn't throw a line in the water somewhere. It's my favorite sport now that I'm no longer able to ski.

Fishing has taken me to many countries of the world, and to many places in this country. I've fished in ponds, creeks, rivers and oceans. I've bait fished, plug fished, lure fished and still fished, using everything from 12-foot bamboo poles to state-of-the-art graphite fly rods. My favorite, though, is fishing with a fly rod in rivers for trout and Atlantic salmon. It's the most challenging and sporting way to fish. It takes a lot of practice to become skillful enough to drop a fly where a trout is lurking, teasing him to strike without spooking him.

I do most of my fishing at my home in Boyne Falls. It's a good stream for Rainbow, Brook and Brown trout. In the spring and summer I fish it in the evenings and can usually catch dinner for the next day. For years, my wife and I have made it our main dish two or three times a week. The kids were raised on it as youngsters, and aren't as fond of fish as Lois and I. Maybe that's because they had to eat it or go hungry.

Fishing partly explains my fondness for Big Sky, Montana, and a reason I sometimes go there when it's not absolutely necessary for business. I keep a few rods and a box of flies there, and usually fish with my son John during visits. The Gallatin and Madison rivers are at Big Sky's doorstep. The Yellowstone River running through America's first national park is also close by. These are great streams for Cutthroat trout. If you happened to see the movie "A River Runs Through It," the fishing scenes were filmed on the Gallatin and witnessed by some of our resort's employees.

Yellowstone National Park was the scene of my greatest fishing embarrassment. I was vacationing there with Lois and two friends from Michigan after spending a few days sightseeing and watching moose at Jackson Hole, Wyoming. Driving through the park, I noticed a bunch of guys fishing shoulder-to-shoulder from the riverbank. Must have been forty of them, all using casting rods.

I wandered down and struck up a conversation. Not one of them was having any luck. No one even had a nibble. I went back, grabbed my fly rod and a couple of flies from the trunk of my car and joined them. Within a couple of minutes I hooked a Cutthroat, and then another. A native with a casting rod came over and asked what bait I was using. I told him it was a dry fly. He checked it out and said, "A dry fly. I'm going to get me one of them," and he raced off in his pickup.

A few minutes later we were cruising through the park. Lois was driving and I was checking out the river. Suddenly I saw a section where the water was boiling. Fish, big fish, were jumping all over the place. I opened the car's trunk, fumbled excitedly getting into my waders, grabbed the rod and literally ran down to the river. I caught a whopper on my first cast, released him, and two casts later had another on the fly. Here was dinner.

Just then a voice close behind me asked, "Mister, are you going to throw that fish back while it's still alive, or am I going to have to arrest you?"

A park ranger was glaring at me. He pointed to a big sign about 10 feet away that said: PROTECTED AREA. NO FISHING PERMITTED. I don't remember ever being more chagrined. I put the fish I'd landed back into the river and apologized profusely.

Not seeing that sign gives you an idea of how excited I can get when I see fish in a feeding frenzy. I still get that way when the May flies are hatching and the fish are jumping everywhere in the waters of the Boyne River at my home. The hatch happens every year on the Boyne in late June or early July and lasts for a week or so. That's a period when my wife knows better than to schedule a dinner out or some other function that would make me miss any part of the hatch.

One year, I was fishing in Norway on the Alta River, a famous Atlantic salmon stream. I hooked a giant, knew it the second he started his run. He was a monster. The fish took me and my guide downstream, battling every inch of the way. It took an hour and a half before the guide finally got him in the net. He was a 47-pounder, the largest Atlantic Salmon caught on a fly rod anywhere in the world in 1969. He was a trophy fish, so magnificent that I decided to take him home and have him mounted. I had him packed in ice and took him to the airport for the flight back home. When I modestly bragged about my record fish (and what fisherman wouldn't on such an occasion?), the airline upgraded my ticket and let him fly first class in the seat next to me. A replica is now in the trophy case in the Eriksen Room at Boyne Mountain.

You're not always successful when you fish for salmon. Many a time I've gone to a famous salmon river and never had a fish rise all week, much less strike my fly. Those trips weren't without pleasure, however. Donning a pair of waders and casting a line where you think a fish is likely to rise is plenty of fun in itself. You're outdoors, breathing in clean air, listening to the sound of rushing water, concentrating on casting to a chosen spot, maybe hearing a bird sing. All of your cares seem to melt away. You're where you want to be and loving every second of it. It's peaceful and tranquil, until a fish rises, of course, and then your adrenaline flows and the excitement begins.

Chasing Atlantic salmon has taken me to many parts of the globe, including Norway, Iceland, Russia, Labrador, New Brunswick and Quebec. Anacosta Island is one of my favorite places to fish for the Atlantic, and where I've had great luck.

The island is about 150 miles long and located at the mouth of the St. Lawrence Seaway. It's part of the Province of Quebec, Canada, and is one of the most beautiful islands

I have ever seen. The island's Jupiter River runs through cliffs that rise two- to three-hundred feet straight up along the edge of the river, solid rock, right down to the water. Gorgeous. You can't believe how beautiful that river is as it winds down through the canyons, like some parts of the Colorado. I don't believe there's a river in the world that's clearer. You can see every fish in the river from the bank, every individual fish before you ever throw a fly in. And you can throw your fly to whichever fish you choose and see him come up and take it. I've caught more salmon in the Jupiter River than in any river in Canada.

In August of 1994, I had the opportunity to fish for salmon at Ted Williams' camp on the Miramichi River in New Brunswick, Canada. Williams, as baseball fans know, was one of the greatest hitters in history, once batting over .400 for the Boston Red Sox. What many people don't know is that he was also one of the top two or three fly fishermen in the world. It was his passion, possibly even more than baseball, and he fished year around. Over the years he has caught more than 2,000 salmon in that river.

One place where the fishing is fabulous but the living is primitive is in Russia. It's a trip you make once in a lifetime if you're lucky. Just getting there is tough — it's thousands of air miles and lots of flight changes. The camp, on the Kola Peninsula near the city of Murmansk, is farther north then Norway. It's on the Poine River and the housing is anything but the Ritz. We lived in tents in 40 degree weather.

My son John went with me on this trip, as he has on many. Between the two of us we caught 70 salmon in a week, weighing up to 18 pounds. The fish had come into the fresh water river to spawn from the Barents Sea, an arm of the North Atlantic.

Except for the natives, few had really fished the river for nearly 50 years. That's because the Russians had a submarine base near Murmansk. Foreign fishing boats weren't allowed within hundreds of miles, so there was no netting in the Barents Sea, and the salmon population thrived. It's much like the Atlantic Ocean was 50 years ago, before netting began off the coast.

When you think about pursuing this king of fish, as I did a number of years ago, it's pretty silly and cost prohibitive to travel from Michigan to Russia, or to any far-flung salmon river. About $8,000 is an average cost for a week, whether you catch a fish or not. So I thought, "Why not have an Atlantic salmon fishery right here at home in Lake Michigan where I could fish for these beauties and so could thousands of others?"

In the late 60's and early 70's, the Michigan Department of Natural Resources was planting the silver Coho and Chinook salmon in the big lake, and they were thriving, creating a whole new fishery for the state. I reasoned that if those salmon made it, the Atlantics should be able to survive, too.

I explained to the DNR that the Boyne River running past my house would be an ideal stream for a plant. After all, if we could raise Coho and Chinook salmons, we should plant Atlantic salmon in the Great Lakes and they would survive as well. Smolts (immature fish about 10 inches long) could be released in the river and easily migrate to Lake Michigan. After lots of objections, including flack from a few salmon "purists" who didn't think this king of fish should be in an "ordinary" river, I got approval from the DNR to go ahead with the experiment at my expense.

I supplied 10,000 smolts we bought from Canada. The DNR supervised the plant amid great fanfare. Newspapers and radio stations reported the story. The smolts were spilled into the river in May and immediately made their way downstream and into the lake. We all had high expectations that many would grow and return annually to reproduce.

Before going ahead with the operation, I had extracted a promise from the DNR to close the river below the dam spillway to all but catch-and-release fishing. The next spring I bought another batch of smolts for planting. From then on, the plan was that the DNR would continue the experiment by stripping the eggs from the females that did manage to return, raise them to smolt size in state hatcheries, and restock the Boyne River.

The project turned out to be a huge disappointment to me. The second year, only a few of the fish returned to spawn. The ones that did became sick and died.

The fish biologists were confused as they tried to find out why these Atlantics didn't survive. Unlike Coho salmon that spawn and die, the Atlantic variety spawn and live to return to the river of their birth to procreate year after year.

When the fish began dying off, the biologists thought that the holding pond I had built just to the side of the dam was too warm. I disproved that theory by digging a deep, cold-water well that kept the pond at an ideal temperature.

I'm the only one that ever said the real cause was pollutants the fish had picked up in Lake Michigan. The Atlantic's silvery color darkens to a reddish hue as they stop eating and begin living off of their body fat. A 20-pound Atlantic can lose as much as half its weight during spawning before returning to the lake, where he'll again grow and put on weight. I reasoned that the fish accumulated the pollutants in ever-increasing amounts the longer they lived, and stored them in their body fat. Because they don't eat when spawning, they have to live off of the body fat — fat that contained high levels of PCB's and other toxic chemicals. So they became diseased and died.

Some of the salmon did live and grow, however. One was caught near Chicago that weighed 18 pounds. About six years after my Boyne River test, 40,000 Atlantics were stocked in the Michigan Pere Marquette and Little Manistee Rivers.

Thinking back, the timing for my experiment was lousy. Lake Michigan was loaded with PCB's and other killer chemicals. Now, the lake's water is much cleaner, and getting better every year because of environmental crackdowns on the use of pesticides and industrial chemical spills.

More than ever I'm convinced that the Atlantics will survive and thrive in Lake Michigan if the DNR devote the time and money to this great fighting species as it has to Coho, Chinook and lake trout. Each year the lake is improving and more Atlantics are living and reproducing.

I'm doubtful if I'll see a bountiful Atlantic salmon fishery in my lifetime. But someday it will become a reality. My regret is I won't be around to share in the excitement. But I'm damned proud that I will have made a significant contribution to it.

Building and maintaining a loyal customer base, one of Kircher's first goals, heavily contributed to the early success of Boyne. However, more than that was needed to turn this Midwestern ski hill into a major resort. Kircher knew this and began planning the events which truly helped Boyne grow – and began the fun and excitement that trips to a Boyne Resort are known for.

Boyne Lodge circa 1950

Growing Pains

As with most new ventures, you walk before you can run. Building a customer base of skiers took time, patience, money and work. Until 1953, when I finally decided to make the move north, I kept active in my auto dealership and trailer lot in Detroit, usually going north to tend the Mountain's business on weekends, but keeping in touch by phone daily. Jim Christianson doubled as manager and bartender the first year. He left Boyne for a job with a radio station in Detroit. Our next manager was a gent who made a fortune in oil well stocks and had moved up north. I told him that the pay was $50 a week."You don't think a millionaire should work for $50 a week, do you?" he asked. "That's what the job pays, and that's all we can afford," I answered. He took the job and seemed to enjoy it immensely.

Chuck Moll joined the company in 1950 as general manager, second in command of the operation. We worked side-by-side and he handled things when I was absent. He was my right hand man, and became my closest friend and confidant. For forty years he contributed more to the growth and success of Boyne USA than I had a right to expect. When he died at age 75 from a sudden and unexpected heart attack, I cried. I felt like a widower at the death of a mate.

In those first few years we had a number of fine employees. Louie and Violet Mangles came out of retirement to run the cafeteria after selling their popular "Louis" restaurant in Boyne City.

After Christianson left, Walter Hardy managed the bar and assisted Victor Gottschalk with the ski school. Walter was an expert skier who had been slated for a berth on the Swiss Olympic ski team until Hitler changed his plans. An avid hunter, Walter was once featured in a story that appeared in state newspapers when his wife shot a deer in their backyard near Detroit, while he had traveled more than 600 miles to the north country without getting a shot.

The Gatlinburg lift business helped finance the Mountain's expansion. We cut new runs, added new lifts and skier facilities as we could afford them. My father had pounded into me the evils of going into debt. So each year at the end of the ski season, we'd pay our outstanding bills, pay the local taxes and the confiscatory 50% or more to the IRS, and see what was left.

Then we'd allocate it to specific projects, for example: $20,000 to expand the lodge, $15,000 for a new lift and new ski run, $5,000 for rental skis and boots, $2,000 for grading the parking lot, etc. Norton sold out his interest in the corporation early, and Christianson didn't particularly care to invest in more stock, so it was my ball game.

I'm damn proud of the fact that I've never borrowed from the federal government or from pension funds. Especially those Small Business Association (SBA) government guarantee loans that were never intended to finance resorts or recreation in the first place. Many of these "loans" never got paid back. Even the interest was forgiven, with the American public picking up the tab.

Boyne Mountain was built entirely with private money, personally backed bank loans, revenues from skiing and from our scenic chairlift in Gatlinburg, Tennessee. We've never gone to the public for a dime.

I've never been shy about charging a fair rate for a good product. Right from the start I decided that Boyne Mountain lift ticket rates were going to be at the top of the scale, despite the advice of friends and associates and quite a few protests from skiers. The rate we charged from day one was $5, and I increased it to keep pace with inflation. My philosophy was that for top dollar I'd give them top quality. That's the best I could do. I reasoned if I did that, people would pay. That's giving you respect, and you're not downgrading your product.

We've never really taken anything out of the business. We've supported the government all these years with 50% or more of all revenue, the rest went back into the business.

In spite of the taxes, we developed the best facilities in the Midwest, and Boyne's ski business began to take off in the early fifties. There was a time when we couldn't build rooms fast enough to handle the skiers who wanted to stay at the resort.

We were getting big crowds on weekends, filling every room we had. Winters up north, once dead, came alive. New motels and restaurants were built and opened, adding to the attraction. Skiers began building chalets and vacation homes, stimulating the economy and increasing our hard-core skier base. About 70% of the skiers came from the Metro Detroit area, most of the rest from Grand Rapids and the Chicago areas. Weekday business was slow, however, barely enough to keep the lifts running except over holidays when kids were on vacation from school.

Two ideas turned midweeks around. Manager Chuck Moll began going after midweek convention and meeting business from associations and various small companies. I came up with the Boyne Mountain Learn-to-Ski Week.

I'm not sure where I got the ski week idea. Maybe from packages being offered by Sun Valley, Stowe and other resorts. Or maybe it just seemed like the logical thing to do to attract business. But I decided to offer the best ski deal anywhere. One with everything included: lodging, meals, lift tickets, ski instruction, taxes and no hidden charges. One all-inclusive, tidy package at a rate hard to pass up-just $49 for the whole package. And we made money on that.

We promoted the learn-to-ski aspect of the ski weeks to the hilt. That's what people wanted. The sport was relatively new and exciting with an element of dare. More and more people wanted to take it up, so we played up the teaching expertise of our Austrian ski instructors and ease of learning. We also touted the weeks as great for family togetherness and fun. For the single crowd, it was the ideal place to find romance. Lots of good-looking girls for good-looking guys. What little advertising we could afford usually featured pictures of beautiful girls riding a chairlift or gathered around a fireplace. That advertising approach attracted the young singles of both sexes.

Kids had their own ski week programs: instruction classes, races, lunches with their Austrian instructors, hot chocolate breaks, movies in the evenings, all sorts of entertainment. They loved it. And everybody eagerly looked ahead to Thursdays when we had ski races for all participants during the day, and an awards banquet at night.

Our Austrian ski instructors were key players in the ski weeks' success and popularity.

They were young, handsome and hand-picked by Othmar Schneider from Austria's Krukenhauser professional skier school. All spoke English, albeit with accents that seemed to delight our guests. They were, of course, excellent teachers who bonded with their skiing students on a first-name basis and mingled with them during meals and in the lounges at night.

At the awards banquets the men dressed in authentic Austrian Lederhosen and the women instructors dressed in their colorful native Austrian garb. They entertained the guests with Bavarian folk songs and traditional Alps music, making the evenings festive and memorable.

The Learn-to-Ski program took off like a rocket. To meet demand we built the Hemlock Chalet and Edelweiss Lodge. Then we added the Boynehof Lodge, connecting it to the main lodge. Then we added another addition to the Edelweiss, doubling its capacity. It wasn't long before we could house over 500 guests, but even that wasn't enough. We kept adding lifts and rooms as fast as we could afford them. Guests who attended one ski week almost always signed up for the next year before leaving, so by the time one ski season ended we were virtually booked to capacity for the next one.

Looking back now, I can hardly believe what we charged for the ski week when we started it. The price for everything – room, lift, three meals daily, and lessons was only $49 per person for five full days. Just to be sure my memory hadn't gone south on me I checked back in our archives and found an old brochure that headlined the price in bold type.

At that time, I was paid $12,000 a year, while Chuck Moll received $8,000 a year and the average Boyne employee made $.90 an hour.

Quite suddenly, the rocket took a nose dive. In the late 60's and early 70's the airlines came out with giveaway fares, particularly on flights from Chicago to Denver. For example,

Chuck Moll bought a round trip ticket from Chicago to Denver for $35 on Ozark Airlines. (We still have the original ticket.) Other major carriers soon slashed prices. And that ended the bulk of our midweek Chicago business, as well as knocking a hole in weekend trade. At those ridiculous rates, it was almost as cheap to go west to the Rockies for the weekend as it was to drive to Boyne.

The cheap fares brought the building boom at Boyne Mountain to an abrupt halt except for lift and trail expansion. I was sure that we could continue to build the weekend business with superior snow, grooming, new lifts, trails and other facilities. However, it was clear I'd have to look elsewhere if I wanted to increase company revenue and assets.

Chuck Moll and his wife, Donna, began attending all sorts of travel and business shows in Chicago and Detroit. They'd set up a booth with hand-made signs promoting Boyne as a great place to combine a business meeting with skiing fun.

Our first legitimate convention group was an association of road contractors. Later that month, Mike O'Neil brought in his bunch of dry cleaners. They were an organized group and Mike was the executive director, who was headquartered in Lansing.For years Mike brought conventions to Boyne and he became a good friend. He was a member of the Capital Club, an exclusive group consisting of directors and executive heads of all sorts of associations. The operating base for these groups chose Lansing, Michigan's capitol, making it easier to lobby the state legislators for their causes.

One day I was doing a bit of lobbying myself with a skiing physician from Traverse City, telling him Boyne was a great place to hold meetings, combining business with pleasure. The doctor's name was Richard Thrilby, a urologist. He got a number of the Traverse City doctors together and they formed the Midwest Medical Association. They held their first meeting at Boyne, returning year after year.

We had a lot of trouble with our waitresses early on. They would go on strike because the doctors wouldn't tip. We had to subsidize the waitresses to keep them on the job. Talk about running a classy five-star hotel. At the end of a ski week, the waitresses would put a bowl with a few dollars in it with the word "tip" on each table. That didn't work very well so Chuck Moll redesigned our dinner check, adding "gratuity" at the bottom. That removed the "help the poor" onus, and people began writing in a tip after each meal. Then we became even more modern, taking the tips and charging them to each person's room. Chuck bought a new fangled cash register that would make up the bill and properly credit each waitress with whatever gratuity they had earned.

Conventions have been the salvation of our midweek summer and winter business ever since.

Bill Flemming, who gained world wide recognition as a sportscaster with ABC television, was best known for hosting ABC's Wide World of Sports. Bill first became acquainted with Everett Kircher in the mid-fifties and has been a fan and close friend ever since. Bill lives near Kircher in northern Michigan and is also a neighbor in Florida.

Through other eyes

Bill Flemming

My first contact with Everett Kircher came in the mid 50s. I had come to Detroit's Channel 4, WWJ-TV, in 1953, and at the time there was a real void of skiing information in the media. The station's sports announcer, Van Patrick, would broadcast maybe 30 seconds about general skiing, snow conditions up north and so forth.

In 1954, Warren Miller, the celebrated ski lecturer and ski cinematographer, came to Detroit as part of the American Youth Hostel series at Ford Auditorium. Warren had watched my television show and called me from his room at the Fort Shelby Hotel. He told me who he was and what he was doing, and wanted to know if I would emcee his two programs.

In return for that I invited him to be on my TV show. He brought a few clips with him, and he was a delightful personality. His clips were funny and I was intrigued with him and his movies. Having emceed his program for two nights, I saw a great potential for that sort of thing for television.

Consequently, I got with our graphic artist, and we decided that on every Thursday night we would put out a pretty extensive ski report, devoting three or four minutes of my 15-minute show to it. Harry Wayne, a talented artist and a fine cartoonist, created little skier caricatures, and he would show these figures skiing at whatever snow depths had been

67

reported to us. With a lot of snow, the skier would be shown waist deep in the stuff, with no new snow or just a dusting, he would appear skiing on hard pan. This feature became very popular, and the station got a lot of mail on it. The Thursday night show enjoyed higher ratings than our shows on other week-nights.

Jim Christianson, who had been one of the original stockholders of the Boyne Mountain ski area, was working as general manager at the Channel 56 educational station in Detroit at the time. He called me about the show and wondered if I would come up and meet Everett Kircher. I then got a call from Chuck Moll, Boyne's general manager, inviting me and my wife, Barbara, to come up to Boyne for the weekend.

It turned out to be one of those perfect winter weekends. I had taken my 16mm Bolex camera along, and did quite a bit of filming. Stein Eriksen, the Olympic gold medalist and world champion, had just come aboard as Boyne's director of skiing, and graciously consented to do his famous flip for my camera. The year was 1955. I found Stein to be one of the most charismatic figures of all the sports celebrities I had met (and still, today, more than 40 years later, I believe Stein to be one of the greatest athletes and sports personalities of our time). When I got back to Detroit, I put the film in slow motion and it made a marvelous feature for my program.

My wife, Barbara, and I spent a great deal of time with Everett that weekend. After a day of skiing and filming, we sat down in the Trophy Room, where a bunch of skiers were having après ski fun, and began talking.

I found Everett to be an absolutely fascinating guy. He not only talked about skiing, and the different styles of skiing, but he was very knowledgeable about the technical side of the sport.

He also was very positive about where skiing was headed, predicting a terrific explosion of skiing here in the Midwest. Up until that time, you either went to Sun Valley, the Rockies, the Wasatch Mountains in Utah, or maybe California. He said, "I'm going to make Boyne a ski capital so these people don't have to spend three of four hundred dollars just for airfare to go skiing. This is the beginning. And I'd really appreciate anything you can do on television in telling people about our conditions up north."

I said that we'd continue to do our ski reports Thursday evenings as long as they were accurate; that the thing that had disturbed a lot of people was that folks at Caberfae and other places would call in and say that the skiing was great. The kids would go up there, and the skiing would be lousy.

Everett said, "Well, if anybody at Boyne ever does that, he's gone." He was very direct about it. "We're not going to tell any untruths. If you ever get any complaints, if we give you a report that says we have six inches of new powder and we don't, I'll find out who gave you that misinformation, and he won't have the opportunity to do it again."

I left Detroit in 1961 and went on to other things, including ABC's Wide World of Sports. I must honestly say that the experience I had with Boyne and conversations with Everett, plus reporting skiing for eight or nine years, was very beneficial to me. I did ski, but never could classify myself as a skier. Yet I was very enthusiastic about the sport, and absorbed all I could about the fun side and the technical side. I knew the difference between the stem Christi, the Arlberg, the reverse shoulder and other skiing nuances.

I also knew about snow conditions and how to describe and explain them — corn snow, hard pack, mashed potatoes, powder and the like. That many sound silly today, but you have to understand that in those days skiing knowledge was somewhat arcane. Reporting was fairly crude. The information network hadn't been set up. So in 1964 when Wide World of Sports got the rights to the Winter Olympics in Innsbruck, I had a leg up, a little bit of an edge in skiing knowledge that I gleaned in those early days and from talking to Everett.

The ski industry owes much to Everett Kircher. It's well documented that he pioneered snowmaking, introduced the Midwest's first chairlift, developed the world's first three-place and four-place chairlifts, brought the first six-place to the United States and was ahead of other American resorts in having his ski school teach the modern, reverse-shoulder method of skiing exclusively.

Of all of his contributions, I think snowmaking had the most profound effect. Once snow was able to be made by other than God Himself, skiing just became the most popular thing in the wintertime. People like Warren Miller and John Jay, I think, would attest to that. Everett really extended the ski season in the Midwest. What used to be sometimes iffy snow conditions in December, January and February, became good conditions in November, December, January, February, March and April — lengthening the season by three months. I remember a number of times when people were skiing at Boyne Mountain and Boyne Highlands up until the first of May. There's little doubt that Everett and his ski resorts, plus his golf courses, brought tremendous vitality to once-stagnant northern Michigan's economy, winter and summer. And the area continues to grow, making it the most popular all-season venue in the Midwest.

Every king deserves a palace, and Kircher is no exception. Helping to design it himself, his log cabin home – and hundreds of untouched surrounding acres – exemplify his love for nature and fishing. Built on the Boyne River, the cabin is located within only a few miles of Boyne Mountain. Everett has been able to watch his family and his resort grow up here.

Log Cabin Home

Moving up north permanently posed the problem of where to live. I needed something larger and more private than Room 12 where I had been staying on weekends. So I had the first major addition built on the lodge with special attention to quarters for me. It was a downstairs unit, with its own kitchen, bathtub and special entrance. I no longer had to walk down the hallway to go in or out. My son John, oldest of my four children, was born while living there.

I began scouting the general area and the nearby towns for an available house or home-site – Boyne Falls, Boyne City, Petoskey and Charlevoix – but none of these populated areas interested me, preferring instead to be in the countryside with some acreage, yet fairly close to Boyne Mountain. If it was on a lake or a stream where I could fish, so much the better.

I went to Walloon Lake, some seven miles north of Boyne, with some realtors. Walloon Lake has been called one of the seven most beautiful lakes in the country. There was a lovely brick home right at the Country Club with a lawn that ran right down to the water. I was tempted. They wanted $40,000 for the place. I quickly changed my mind. That was like four million in those days.

Lake Charlevoix, about 17 miles from the Mountain, was another possible site. I could have bought land there called Hemingway Pointe, named after the famous writer who spent many of his boyhood summers there. They wanted $50,000 for the 80 acres. Years later, just a small lot there cost twice as much.

My search for a permanent place to live continued for weeks. Most nights after work and site hunting, I'd usually find myself fishing for trout on the Boyne River, less than two miles away from the Mountain.

I'd have to go through an unsightly mess to get down to the spot in the river I liked to fish. The locals, who normally fished the river in the daytime, used the place as a dump for all sorts of garbage. After getting rid of their trash, they would walk down a little trail to the river and fish the hole in the daytime. I'd take a different path in the evening to fish, often having to crawl on my hands and knees under a tangle of brush and discarded junk to get to a special spot in the stream where I could fly fish.

Because of all the undergrowth and overhanging trees on both sides of the river, I'd have to put on waders and climb down into the stream to throw a fly. Keeping the line from getting hung up in the trees and undergrowth was a constant challenge and helped me hone my casting skills considerably.

One night I was sitting there on my favorite log, resting, when I asked myself, "Why am I looking at Walloon Lake and other places when this is where I always end up? Why a lake when a trout stream is my primary interest?"

The river property was owned by Consumers Power Company and they sold me a 160 acre parcel for about $5,000 with the condition that I had to clean up the area. I bought another 500 adjoining acres from Consumers that included a lake formed by the dam, the dam and the power plant with its generators intact. Originally, the plant had provided the electricity for Boyne Falls and Boyne City. When the towns became more populated and demands for power increased, they abandoned it, bringing power in for the communities over transmission lines from other generating sources.

I didn't realize it at the time, but in buying the property I got an unexpected bonus. Because of the energy scare of the 1970's, the government encouraged reactivating dormant hydroelectric power plants. We reopened the Boyne River plant and it has since provided significant amounts of power to Boyne Mountain in recent years.

Fortunately, I bought the property before the Wetlands Act. I had a twenty foot wide corridor of brush and scrub tress cleaned out on one side of the river for over a mile, running down to the lake where we had a little picnic area. It was thick as a jungle. We filled the low spots in the cleared out area and seeded the corridor with bent grass — making a great path for my golf cart. The DNR would put me in jail if I even thought of doing something like that now.

The site I selected for the house was on a ridge about one hundred feet from the river, near enough to see the fish jump. I ordered much of the building materials for the house from the South. I purchased three old log homes in Tennessee, had them dismantled, and they became the exterior walls of my new home. Many of the timbers were up to 35 feet long and eight inches thick. I had a gondola car full of Tennessee crab orchard stone shipped here to Boyne, too. It's a beautiful, non-porous stone which can be used in outdoor patios up North because it won't absorb moisture.

John Norton had a Japanese architect design the house, following my rough plans. Imagine a Japanese architect reconstructing a log home. We had a lot of laughs over that.

I'll never move from that home. It's been added to a number of times. I have a hunting and fishing room where I tie flies, sharpen arrows and store my hunting and fishing gear. The lawn in front of the house slopes down to the river. After a day's work in the spring and summer, I often slip down to the stream in my golf cart to catch some Browns, Rainbows or Brook trout for dinner, clean them and we have a family feast — fresh fish being my favorite.

Our home has been a great place to raise a family. We've been able to have horses, cats, hunting dogs, even a pet raccoon. Except for a couple of meadows, the property is wooded, providing good habitat for deer and other wildlife. The kids have learned to fish, hunt and sail without leaving the property. Being so close to the Mountain, they were able to learn to ski early, becoming experts while still in grade school.

During the hunting season, I can get my limit of ducks and geese from my lake. With that and other game, and the produce from the garden I plant every year, my family and I could live off the land if necessary. I love all four seasons of the year here in northern Michigan and can't think of another place I'd rather live.

Luckily, my wife can't either.

John Clark first became involved with Everett Kircher in the mid fifties when Kircher bought Boyne Highlands. He has since served as Boyne USA's corporate attorney and has been intimately involved with the growth of the resort properties.

Through other eyes

John Clark

For many years, I have had the privilege and pleasure to serve as Boyne's corporate attorney and personal attorney for Everett Kircher and his family. I also have become a close friend.

When Everett decided to buy Harbor Highlands, I became involved in the legal work. The ski area hadn't been open for two seasons and had amassed considerable debt. The stockholders, most of them Harbor Springs and Petoskey residents, had decided to sell and they established an asking price that was agreeable to Everett. The asking price, however, did not include payment of all outstanding debts.

After checking over the creditor list, Everett said, "I'll pay their asking price, but I want to pay off their bills, too. That way all of the shareholders will recover their full investments." I pointed out that wasn't necessary, but he insisted.

"Look, Jack, I'd like to go into the area with everybody feeling happy about the deal and about Boyne. This way the stockholders won't be losing a dime, the creditors won't either, everybody will be happy."

I've worked out many sales agreements, but this was the first and probably the only one where a buyer showed such generosity. Upon reflection, it was a brilliant move on Everett's part. It surely established a lot of goodwill and made a bunch of instant friends for Boyne.

Before beginning to develop and expand the area, Everett decided that he wanted to buy about 600 more acres on the ridge just to the north of Harbor Highlands. The property was owned by the state. We contacted the Michigan Conservation Commission (now the DNR). They refused to sell but would consider a land swap.

There were 1,248 acres in 12 parcels that the state might take in a trade. The parcels adjoined other state lands or were suitable for parks or other public usages. We took the list and property descriptions and, one by one, managed to arrange options to buy all of the 12 parcels. I accompanied Everett and Chuck Moll, Boyne's manager, to Lansing to help arrange the land swap.

The Conservation officials readily agreed to the trade. The state got all 1,248 acres. We had expected to get about 600 acres, but came away with 903. It was a win-win situation for all. The state got additional land that the public could use, plus a ski and golf resort that would certainly promote tourism and provide jobs.

Boyne got what it wanted. One of the officials, seeking yet another solid reason to approve the trade, asked Everett if the new resort would help reduce local juvenile delinquency. "I'm not sure," Everett responded. "But it may help concentrate it in one place."

Skiing's popularity heated up in the late '50s, particularly in the Midwest where winter-bred cabin fever drove folks to seek outdoor excitement. Like McDonald's restaurants, Midwest ski areas began springing up everywhere, some as private enterprises, others as small-town community endeavors. Most had rope tows or some sort of surface lift or two. Few, if any, had chairlifts or snowmaking equipment. The lodges were little more than warming huts with restrooms. Here, Kircher relays how he leveraged that competition to his advantage and ensured Boyne's success.

Boyne Highlands circa 1963.

Onward and Upward

In 1962 the Michigan Chamber of Commerce reported that the state had 174 operating alpine ski areas. In "Boyne Country", the name we coined to pinpoint our general area in the northwestern part of the state, a number of neighboring areas competed with Boyne Mountain for the skier's dollar: Avalanche in Boyne City; Walloon Hills and Thunder Mountain a few miles northeast of Boyne; Mt. McSauba of Charlevoix; and Harbor Highlands and Nub's Nob, both of Harbor Springs.

All this competition concerned me until I reasoned that this offered more of an opportunity than a threat. If I stayed ahead of the pack in lifts, snowmaking and ancillary facilities, many of the ski areas would become training grounds for Boyne.

At Boyne Mountain we already had five chairlifts, a T-bar, J-bar and two rope tows by 1960 — about triple the lift capacity and skiing terrain of any other Midwestern area. No one could touch us for challenging runs. And looking 10 years or more down the road, I felt that Boyne Mountain would not run out of the kind of ski terrain that would be needed to satisfy the growing ranks of skiers and the ever-increasing competition.

What really galled me was how many of the new areas got their initial financing with little or no personal obligations. Chuck Moll had done some investigating and had learned that the Small Business Administration (SBA) of the federal government was loaning the money to fund ski areas by guaranteeing loans in a reckless way and ostensibly in violation of common business practices.

To get an SBA-backed loan you were supposed to apply for one at a lending institution. It was to loan the money at a reasonable rate of interest, and the SBA would guarantee 90% of the total. The bank or savings and loan would have only 10% of the loan at risk, an amount they would normally cover by demanding some sort of collateral or acceptable personal guarantee. The 90% collateral was U.S. money.

Chuck Moll had discovered that the SBA was allegedly loaning money for ski operations in cases where borrowers couldn't get loans for their projects from a bank or S&L — presumably because the lendee aspirant couldn't or wouldn't meet the institution's financial requirements.

I found this hard to believe, but decided to check it out. We had already been granted a $750,000 loan from a local bank for expansion purposes, so we weren't after the money, but thought it would be a good idea to pretend that we were. Together, Chuck and I visited an SBA office. Our conversation with the SBA officer went something like this:

ME: I'd like to borrow $750,000 to expand Boyne's ski operations.

SBA: Really. Has a lending institution agreed to advance you the money.

ME: No. We tried a lot of banks, but they think that ski resorts are too risky.

SBA: OK. You qualify. How much would you like to borrow?

ME: $750,000.

SBA: Can you put up any collateral or personally guarantee the loan

in case you default?

ME: Not really. And I don't feel that I can afford to. The ski business is

risky — dependent on weather, you know. Pledging my personal assets

wouldn't be fair to my family.

SBA: Well, it is a risky business. You qualify.

Chuck and I walked out, astounded. We could hardly believe it. Here was a government agency loaning out millions of taxpayers' dollars recklessly and irresponsibly. In effect, it was unfairly subsidizing businesses that would compete against entrepreneurs that took personal risks and were privately financed.

Chuck had hidden a tape recorder in his jacket, so we had a record of the entire conversation with the SBA officer. I wasn't about to let the matter drop, and the tape would expose this taxpayer rip-off, probably running into billions of dollars, if our experience was typical. The right people in government had to be told how this bureaucracy was operating.

Gerald Ford, then a member of the U.S. House of Representatives, often skied at Boyne. He came up to Boyne Mountain for the Christmas holidays with his family a few weeks after our SBA meetings. I called him and said, "I have a Christmas present for you, Jerry."

Chuck and I played the tape for him in my office and asked what we should do about the situation. "Nothing," he said. "Just walk away from it, like I'm going to do. Those bureaucrats in Washington can be real s.o.b.'s. You cause them trouble and they'll retaliate in ways you won't believe. They could sic the IRS, the EPA, OSHA and who knows who on you. Expose them and they'll make your life miserable." I took Jerry's advice and let the matter drop, but those sweetheart SBA giveaways have left a bitter taste in my mouth ever since.

With Boyne Mountain doing well and skiing on the upswing, I figured that it was time to make another move. The Harbor Highlands ski area in Harbor Springs had started up in 1955 and was expanded in 1958-59, with stockholders from Petoskey, Harbor Springs and area resorters putting up the capital. It was just 25 miles from Boyne Mountain and was especially appealing to me, having an extraordinarily fine range of hills, by far the best in the lower peninsula, with a vertical of over 550 feet, 50 feet more than at Boyne Mountain.

Only five runs had been cut, and they extended less than halfway to the top of the ridge. Uphill transportation consisted of a poma-lift and four rope tows. A small day lodge with a bar and restaurant had been built at the base of the hill. However, the owners had run out of funds and amassed considerable debt, forcing them to close down. They hadn't opened for the previous two years, and the area was up for sale.

There were 27 Harbor Highlands stockholders, headed by a local mink farmer, O. Brager-Larsen. Chuck Moll and Jack Clark, Boyne's attorney and a close friend of mine, checked out the vital statistics. Mr. Brager-Larsen and his fellow stockholders quoted what I thought was a fair price and we closed the deal. I was pleased with the purchase and especially pleased that the sellers and their creditors hadn't lost any money on their investment. But the land acquired wasn't nearly what I'd need to build the large year-around ski and summer resort I envisioned.

I'd learned the hard way that I'd better lock up all the adjoining land I wanted before I started to develop the facilities — and figured it would take about a year before I'd begin

anything except the planning. Otherwise, I'd be at the mercy of the property owners —
they would have smelled money, and the asking price would escalate by about ten times the
current value of the land the day we started clearing slopes or laying building foundations.
We negotiated a number of buys and secured leases with options to buy on over 2,000
surrounding acres. We also worked out a land swap with the state DNR for over 900
nearby acres.

One critical piece of property at the top of the mountain, where I planned some major
runs, wasn't for sale at any price. It was owned by a retired dentist who had practiced for
years in Harbor Springs — a Dr. Graham. He didn't need the money. And he was especially fond of his property. It was part of a "pioneer farm" that he developed as a hobby. He'd
built a log cabin down in a hollow behind the mountain ridge, and that's where he'd spend
his leisure time. Out in front of the cabin he had a hitching post. He'd tether a horse to the
post, and the horse would walk in a circle, dragging a plow or cultivator. Each year he'd
plant a garden on the tilled soil. He loved this pioneer farm, and although he'd had offers
to sell a portion to the former owners of Harbor Highlands, he always refused. He wasn't
very fond of some of the stockholders.

I visited Dr. Graham, hoping to get him to change his mind about selling the acreage
at the top side of the mountain range. We had a number of friendly talks at his farm, and
found we had a lot in common in our love of nature and history. Finally, I persuaded him
to visit me at my house in Boyne Falls. I pointed out the old logs and timbers I'd used in
building it, and some of my early American furnishings. He appreciated old things, and took
a liking to me. He finally agreed to sell me the parcel at the top of the mountain that I needed. But there was a stipulation: to buy it I had to promise to build a sizable mound at the
very top and name it Graham's Peak. From there Dr. Graham would have a commanding

view of Lake Michigan and of the land below that he loved.

The top of the ridge was the highest point in the lower peninsula. We cleared a part of the mountain top to make room for lift terminals, took the logs, dragged them into a pile and covered them with dirt. The pile of dirt was built up to a height of 50 feet. It was an ugly eyesore and I hated it from day one but Dr. Graham was pleased. He often climbed the mound to look out over the big lake and the forest below.

When he died a few years later, I visited his heirs and told them I had wanted to knock down the mound, but would replace it with a church and name it Graham Chapel. I had architectural renderings made of the proposed building: a beautiful edifice of stone and cedar, a fitting monument to the memory of Dr. Graham. You'd have thought that the heirs would be delighted, replacing an ugly pile of dirt with a lovely chapel. I was flabbergasted when certain of the heirs objected. They would agree if I gave them and their families free lifetime passes to ski and golf. I didn't need their permission, but in deference to the fond memories I had of the doctor, and of the promise I had made to him, I agreed and gave the heirs the passes.

Graham Chapel has worked out wonderfully. It's really a lovely church in a beautiful outdoor setting — high up on the mountain, surrounded by woods and serene with some great views. Its pews hold about 60 people without crowding. I'm very proud of it.

My two oldest children, John and Amy, were both married there. I expect that when the time comes, my other two, Stephen and Kathryn, will want to be married there as well. Many other couples from the community have spoken their vows in the Chapel. During the winter, we make it available to skiers for Sunday morning services. They ride the lift up, park their skis outside and take to the slopes after church. And we always have an Easter sunrise service there – it's become a tradition.

Another parcel I wanted for what was to become Boyne Highlands was a 40-acre section just north of where I intended to build the main lodge. It was owned by a man who had lived there in a shack, but had abandoned it and moved to Florida.

Mr. Brager-Larson tracked him down in Florida, convincing him to sell. Undeveloped property in the area at that time was going for $100 or less per acre. I got it for an inflated $1,000 per acre — a $40,000 whack. Later, we built a deer pen on a portion of the 40, and the rest became part of the Robert Trent Jones Heather golf course.

Developing the Highlands was hard work but a lot of fun. I finally had sufficient land to cluster buildings conveniently close to the ski slopes. The main Highlands Inn, a striking, Bavarian/Old-English, three-story lodge, was the resort's first building, and a great opportunity for me to play architect. My sketches, made from photographs of English and other European buildings that had impressed me on trips overseas, were refined by Boyne's architect, Jim Livingston.

I'm pleased to say that our guests have found the lodging quite impressive. It was renovated and updated in 1992. Rooms have been appointed with coordinated drapes and bedspreads, lovely carpeting, designer case goods, colorful wallpaper and state-of-the-art bathroom fixtures, all done by the Boyne Design Group, Inc., which my daughter, Kathryn, heads up.

In its October 1995 issue, *SKI Magazine* rated Boyne Highlands one of the top five ski resorts in North America for excellence of lodging, publishing the results from an extensive survey of its readers. Sharing the top five were: Whistler/Blackcomb, British Columbia; Sun Valley, Idaho; Steamboat, Colorado; and Sugarloaf, Maine. Rounding out the top ten were Aspen, Colorado; Schweitzer Mountain, Idaho; Telluride, Colorado; Heavenly Valley, California; and Mammoth Mountain, Colorado.

During the planning stages of Boyne Highlands, as my wife and I were riding up the double-place chairlift at Boyne Mountain with our six year old son, John, squeezed in between us I thought, "Wouldn't it be great to have a three-passenger chairlift instead of just a two? A triple?"

Maybe someone else had the same thought, but no one had done anything about it up to that point. It was a case of the old habit syndrome. People too often get locked into old habits. It's a comfortable feeling. Ski areas around the world were apparently comfortable with doubles, and continued to order and install them. But the triple idea wouldn't leave me.

I called Riblet, a leading manufacturer of chairlifts, and asked them to engineer and build two of them for me, saying it shouldn't be too difficult a project. It wouldn't be a case of having to reinvent the wheel, just a matter of improving it. They agreed, and when Boyne Highlands made its debut in 1963, skiers were greeted with the world's first triple chairlifts. Those original two are still in operation at the Highlands today.

They were so well received that I didn't want to stop there. I contacted Bob Heron of the lift-building Heron company, and asked him to manufacture a four-place lift for Boyne Mountain. He took the challenge and the lift was installed at the resort in 1969. It was the world's first four-passenger lift, impressive enough in concept to elicit visits by ski area representatives from Austria's Doppelmayr, the world's foremost manufacturer of trams and lifts.

From the outset my goal was to make the Highlands a winter and summer resort. Skiing would take care of the winter months. Golf had to be the answer to the late spring, summer and fall seasons. It would be the main attraction for meeting and convention groups — a draw that would allow me to keep our key winter staff employed year around. Not for a moment did I think that golf in itself would be profitable here in our limited five-month season. It seemed to be the only avenue I had, and something that had to be done. And done right, or not at all.

The most famous and respected golf course architect at the time was Robert Trent Jones Sr. We contacted him, struck a deal, and the Heather golf course was the result. It was dedicated in 1968 and by 1971 it became one of *Golf Digest's Top 100 Golf Courses in the United States.* To my knowledge, Boyne Highlands was the first ski area in the country to build a championship golf course.

The Heather was the catalyst that triggered the golf boom in northwest Michigan, now widely known as "America's Summer Golf Capital." Among some 40 courses in this part of the state in 1995 (multiplying by about half a dozen each year, it seems) Boyne owns six 18-hole courses at the Highlands and the Mountain, and a spectacular 27-hole layout on the cliffs of Lake Michigan at the Bay Harbor Resort in Petoskey, Michigan.

Both Boyne Mountain and Boyne Highlands were doing well in the late 60s, with little indication of slowing down. Our cash flow was good, we had money in the bank. Even our midweek business was fairly strong, thanks in a large part to our ability to attract convention business and the popularity of our Learn-To-Ski Weeks.

We had plenty of local competition for weekend business, however, from Nubs Nob, located just across the valley from the Highlands, and from three other local ski areas: Avalanche Mountain at Boyne City, Walloon Hills and Thunder Mountain, the latter two being just a few miles east and west of Boyne Mountain.

None of these four competitors had lodging, except for a dozen or so small rooms at Nubs Nob, so they couldn't offer all-inclusive ski weeks. They survived solely on weekend lift ticket revenue and had no summer business.

Nubs Nob was developed and owned by "Nub" Sarns, former sailor and boat builder, and by his wife, Doris. They had one double chairlift, a Poma-lift and several rope tows, and the Nob had become the area of choice for Harbor Springs and Petoskey families, largely by offering bargain-basement family season passes. The locals had developed a strong loyalty to Nubs — a loyalty that I found difficult to change, even after Boyne Highlands became the # 1 ski resort in the Midwest. This didn't concern me, however.

Avalanche, Walloon Hills and Thunder Mountain all lived on the financial edge. Although they enjoyed local patronage, they didn't have the capital to keep up with the demands of the more sophisticated skier. They had to offer much lower lift ticket rates to attract enough skiers to break even or turn a modest profit, and a poor snow season would really hurt. But those skiers always looking for the lowest prices — and there are and always will be thousands of them, believe me — were the ones that kept them afloat.

When you're surrounded by competitors with rock-bottom rates, and you charge more, you look like the bad guy. I felt that if I could buy out these areas, I could get prices to a level that would make the areas profitable by providing new chairlifts and better base facilities.

Avalanche had been started as a Boyne City community project. It was sold to a dentist, Dr. David Cook of Toledo, Ohio. Walloon Hills and Thunder Mountain had been started by former employees of Boyne after securing an SBA loan. I made separate bids to buy each one, offering $500,000 for each. The principals were happy to sell.

After acquiring Avalanche, I saw no reason to keep it operating. My staff removed its lifts, and we deeded the mountain and property to Boyne City. It's been used for community activities and for hiking, sledding and mountain biking ever since.

We had been especially successful in promoting junior racing and ski club racing at the Mountain and Highlands. In doing so we created a monster. Our recreational skiers would call up to ask if racing was scheduled for a particular day. A "yes" answer would drive them away. Finally, it got to the point where we foresaw having more junior racers than recreational skiers, a sure road to insolvency.

Thunder Mountain had some steep runs, ideal for holding slalom and giant slalom races. The obvious move was to hold nearly all racing there. By concentrating club and junior racing at Thunder, we were able to limit nearly all of the runs at the Mountain and Highlands to recreational skiing only, thus avoiding clashes between racers and recreational skiers and eliminating chopped up ski runs. The recreational skiers saluted us for the move and began avoiding Thunder Mountain altogether. Before long we only had the racers there. That, combined with expansion at the Highlands and Mountain, forced me to close Thunder. The racers by themselves couldn't support it.

Walloon Hills was a nice little ski area, popular with families. We removed their double chair and installed a quad and surface tows, as we had done at Thunder. At Walloon we also expanded the lodge. But after the record ski season of 1968, skiing plateaued and then bottomed out. The continued expansion of runs and lifts at the Mountain and the Highlands made Walloon and Thunder redundant.

After removing the lifts, we donated Walloon to a non-profit group to run as a recreational area for the physically and mentally disadvantaged. It's now called Challenge Mountain. My wife, Lois, was one of the founders of the organization, and Boyne helps to support it with proceeds from a share of the revenue of the Jimmy Huega Express that we sponsor annually at Boyne Mountain.

I'm keeping Thunder in reserve in the event there's another great boom in winter recreation. And there well could be one if snowboarding continues to grow as it has in the past five years. Thunder Mountain would make an ideal area for snowboarding. If I thought that the "boarders" would accept Thunder as their own, I might reopen it just for them. Doing so would make me a hero with downhill skiers and avoid the clashes between the two groups. It's only a thought, and probably won't happen. But anything's possible — so I intend to keep my powder dry.

Editor's Note: Boyne USA provides unrestricted snowboard access on all of the resorts' slopes. In addition, both Michigan resorts feature monstrous groomed half-pipes and have added more waves and table-top elements on which boarders can perfect their techniques.

Margie Germo our first skating instructor.

Two instructors giving a lesson at Boyne circa 1950.

DIPLOMA

THIS IS TO CERTIFY THAT

Jim O'Brien

IS AN *advanced* SKIER AND
HAS GONE THROUGH STEIN ERIKSEN
SKI SCHOOL AT BOYNE MOUNTAIN

January 13th 1956
DATE

Recognition for graduating from the ski school.

The first chairlift in the midwest.

Emil Allay, the French racer, giving a lesson to his son.

Everett's daughter
Kathy Kircher.

Family picture at John and Jessica's wedding.

Amy Kircher in the Florida sunshine.

Lois, Everett and John Kircher.

Hilda Kircher's 90th birthday party with
Amy, Everett and Tyler.

Kathy shows that fly fishing talent runs
in the Kircher family.

Everett at home at Boyne Falls.

Donna and Chuck Moll.

Everett looks over his Gatlinburg lift.

Ski enthusiasts in the early days.

Othmar Schnieder

Othmar Schneider's famous ski school.

Freidl Pfeiffer head of Aspen Ski School, Stein Eriksen
and Kircher at the second pro race in America. The first
was at Aspen the week earlier.

Governor William Miliken and his wife Helen.

Skiers dream of slopes covered with soft snow in which they can make crisp, tight turns – turns that push the snow gently away from the skis. In dreams, these slopes are without the threat of an ice patch that can quickly cause a skier to lose control and hit the ground in a hurry. As a skier, Kircher had this same dream and, from the beginning, fought a war with nature – determined to minimize ice on his slopes.

Then There Was Ice

When we'd get a snowfall at Boyne in the early years, the first order of business was packing the slopes. Otherwise, a foot of new, unpacked snow would be lost — and in a couple of hours your slopes would be down to the hard pack. The fresh stuff would all be pushed off to the side of the runs in piles or end up in the woods. At first we'd shovel it back onto the slopes by hand, but that didn't work very well — you could only toss a shovel full of snow just so far.

A pretty simple solution was a labor-saving invention maybe a couple of hundred years old. A coal chute! I bought the longest ones I could find, had them welded together and elevated to a required height. Our snowmakers, maintenance crew, ski patrolmen and all the volunteers we could talk into working by offering free lift tickets, would deposit the reclaimed snow from the woods to the center of a run. It still took plenty of work, but got the job done easier and faster than before.

The snow in the woods was mostly virgin snow, usually very light in moisture content. It still had to be spread around and packed or it would be back in the woods after a few skier runs. So I'd close the slope for the day, hoping the snow would harden up overnight. The next day we'd usually open it for limited skiing. Our loud speaker system would blare out "Hemlock is open for two hours." And the rush would be on.

After a fresh snowfall it was law that nobody skied until the runs were packed top to bottom. The problem with that dictatorial decree, other than grumbles by skiers eager to hit the slopes, was that no mechanical packers had yet been invented. You had to invent your own from scratch. So the snow had to be packed by the skiers, on foot with skis.

Before the lifts officially opened, the ski patrol would ride up and sidestep down, foot-by-foot. There would always be volunteers to help to hurry up the operation. As soon as a run was packed we'd start on another until all the slopes were open for free skiing. Not an ideal operation.

My first attempt at developing a mechanical packer was a contraption I sketched out and sent down to my auto dealership to have built. Don Thomas, one of my car salesmen and an original member of the Boyne ski patrol, headed up the project. The packer consisted of six-foot wooden slats mounted around bicycle wheels which rotated on an axle. Of course, you had to have something to pull it.

Chuck Moll managed to uncover an army surplus Weasel we could buy. It was our first vehicle worth anything in the snow and it had plenty of power. It was a snowcat-type thing, with treads similar to those on tanks. The 10th Mountain Division used them to fight the

Germans in World War II.

My packing "invention" didn't begin to do the job — much too light to compress the snow adequately. Oil drums hooked together, filled with water and pulled by the Weasel did a better job. It still took much too long to pack a run and would leave unpacked ridges between the barrels.

A far bigger problem, and one harder to cope with, was iced-up slopes. Every time we had a rain or bad thaw, followed by normal freezing temperatures, we'd get ice and always will. As everyone knows, skiers like their ice in a glass, not on a ski hill. When a mountain ices up it's "good-bye skiers."

Patches of ice often occur where there is heavy skier traffic or in spots where a snow-gun has misfired. Hit an ice patch during a turn and Wham! You're down. Our crew used to hatchet out the patches until we got more sophisticated by using bulldozers, choppers, rakes and drags my staff and I designed and built.

Fixing ice took more time and experience than did learning to make quality snow. Western ski resorts never have had ice problems like Midwestern resorts. The mountains seldom experience thaws and at the skiing elevations in the winter nighttime temperatures are always at freezing.

After years of experience we have mastered the snow conditioning art. When a slope ices up we use giant tillers that break the ice into small particles and fold it into the softer snow below. We knock down the moguls and add a generous topping of new, man-made snow, leaving a smooth, ice-free, mogul-less slope, the likes of which Mother Nature can't duplicate without man's help.

Today's skiers are spoiled. They don't want even a trace of a ripple on a slope. But they talk about the thrills of "deep powder," which most of them probably haven't skied, and couldn't anyway without wider, softer skis.

I call powder skiing the industry's glamorous lie. All resorts pack their slopes, leaving maybe a couple of runs with moguls that only a few skiers dare to challenge anyway. The real powder devotees have to resort to helicopter transportation to some off-area mountain, or climb to an undesignated run. It's only been since the early '80s that European ski areas pack and groom their runs. They do it now because that's what the skiing public demands.

At our Boyne resorts we concentrate our towers and stationary snow guns at the top of our runs, doubling up the amounts of man-made snow we make there. That's because every time we groom we scrape off about four inches of snow and it winds up at the bottom. But this grooming, which we do religiously every night, costs almost as much as snowmaking. A new groomer costs about $150,000, and lasts only three years. We have four of them at Boyne Mountain, partially explaining why lift tickets cost as much as they do.

Even at the price we charge for lift tickets, Boyne Mountain has been a losing proposition for the last four or five years to the tune of $1,500,000 annually. We've been able to keep it operating only because it's subsidized by revenues from Boyne Highlands, our western resorts and the Gatlinburg scenic chairlift. How long this situation exists only time will tell. We're doing everything possible to reduce costs wherever we can.

One area where we've been quite successful in cost containment is in snowmaking. Compared to the typical air and water machines, our patented fan gun snow machines use one-twelfth the energy of other types. To convert 40 gallons of water to snow, we use 50 cubic feet per minute (CFM) of compressed air. The other types use 600 CFM — and generating compressed air is the most expensive part of snowmaking.

Cost containment, without sacrificing service or quality of product, has always been my number one priority – and it always will be.

Kircher learned early on that to be successful you have to push the limits, try things others haven't even thought of, become an industry leader. He did this with Boyne by always searching for ways to be the best – have the best lodges, the best ski instructors, the best facilities and even the best snow. In the 1950s, Kircher began a life-long search to create skiable snow, even when Nature did not provide. Once again, he succeeded.

Boyne Mountain circa 1950

Helping Mother Nature

Snow is one of Mother Nature's greatest gifts. As a child I loved it when winter came and snow covered the ground. Winter became my favorite season of the year. And for nearly fifty years I've depended upon it for my livelihood.

To a ski resort operator there's nothing as depressing as snowless slopes — particularly when the Christmas-New Year's season nears. That's when we do 30% or more of our annual business. Ski-weekers will have packed the rooms. All of the area motels for thirty miles around will be displaying No Occupancy signs. You'll have 10,000 skiers eager to line up at the ticket windows. But without snow, the cash registers will be silent and your customers will be heading home, or scurrying to find it somewhere else.

Although Boyne Mountain and Boyne Highlands are both located in the Midwest's snowbelt, and greatly benefit from lake effect snow, the snowless scenario gives me nightmares every year.

Starting in November, my first act every winter morning, even before coffee, is to check the weather. We'll almost always have a good snowstorm around November fifteenth — deer-hunting season. From that point on I'll be on the weather watch, always expecting an early thaw and getting one more often than I care to remember.

Praying doesn't help. Shaking my fist at the sky and You-Know-Who doesn't help. Whenever he feels like it, God is going to play a dirty trick on me, and there's nothing I can do about it.

Then in 1953, I somehow must have gotten into God's good graces. Vic Chmielewski, my area manager who was with Boyne from the beginning, had read something about artificial snowmaking at Grossinger's resort in the Catskill Mountains. He said he'd like to go there and find out about it. He made the trip and described the operation. They were spraying a stream of water between compressed air jets. Presto! Man-made snow.

Vic had owned a gas station before he came to work for Boyne. So I said, "Vic, you still have a compressor? Okay. We've got hoses and sprinkler nozzles, and can get water from the faucet. Let's see what we can do."

We cobbled up a little tripod stand with a center water jet and an air jet on either side. Then we criss-crossed compressed air into the stream. It worked. We made snow right off. Right then my course was charted. I would chase after snowmaking with the fervor of Ahab hunting Moby Dick.

It was reported in a news article that an engineer named Troplano was working for the Larchmont Engineering Company of Lexington, Massachusetts, a firm that manufactured sprinkling systems, when he first observed snow being made. It occurred on a cold morning when blowing the air out of the system. His brother Joe, a skier, recognized the possibilities of the discovery, and they took the idea to Grossinger's in the Catskills.

Other ski resorts were quick to see the potential and began to experiment with snowmaking. We heard about one in Wisconsin — Wilmot, a small ski area located between Chicago and Milwaukee.

Chuck Moll and I decided to go there and check out their system. We drove to Ludington, Michigan, and took the car ferry across Lake Michigan to Milwaukee at 5 a.m.

Wilmot was a really primitive ski area back then. Their lodge was furnished with old car seats. The men's john consisted of a rain gutter sloping down a wall to a hole in the ground. The snowmaking system was equally primitive, but it obviously worked. That was the first time I saw an entire slope covered with man-made snow.

Their snowmaking apparatus consisted of air and water pumped through aluminum pipes lying along the ground with lawn sprinklers attached. The sprinklers had to be watched every second when making snow. If one stuck, they got slush or a stream of water. There were wind problems, too.

When we got back home from Wisconsin we began experimenting with all sorts of snowmaking equipment. It was trial and error – learn as you go. That's the way it was with many of my skiing projects. No science existed – you invented it as you went along.

Moveable duck-billed guns on tripods with air and water fed through surface hoses worked well at Boyne early on. At one time, I had more than 500 duck-bill stations operating at the Mountain. To supply air for all of these stations, we used to rent huge, noisy diesel air compressors you could hear for miles. Ultimately, we went from diesels to electrical compressors. Millions of gallons of water were required, so we had to dig wells, build reservoirs and pumping stations.

Surface air and water lines had to be buried to remove dangerous hazards and alleviate most freezing problems. We developed larger snowmakers with multiple jets, mounting these on wheeled chassis' easy to move around. Fans were added to improve snow quality, making it lighter and drier by breaking water droplets into mist.

I'm convinced that our man-made snow is now as good or better than natural snow. It's more durable because it contains more moisture. One inch of machine-made snow is equivalent to a foot of natural snow in moisture content, durability and density. Therefore, it packs better, lasts longer and provides a more consistent surface than the natural stuff.

I have no idea how many thousands of hours I've spent with Vic and others on our staff, experimenting with nozzles, pressures, water volume, humidity levels and all of the other things that go into making snow. A friend recently reminded me of how consumed I was with the effort, citing a time when I was up on the Mountain in near-zero temperatures, and actually sweating as I adjusted air and water volumes while cursing if a gun dared to make slush.

Finally, after years of re-engineering and refinements, we developed the *Boyne Snowmaker*, later named the *Highlands Snow Gun*. I had it patented and licensed.

The gun is very efficient, using less electricity and less air per pound of water than most other systems. And it will make snow at 30 degrees Fahrenheit whenever humidity levels are low enough. Most competitive systems have difficulty making decent snow at temperatures higher than 28 degrees. The Highlands Snow Gun is being used today at hundreds of ski areas around the world — solid testimony to its efficiency.

As long as I'm breathing, I'll still be working on snowmaking improvements. We've been erecting towers and mounting our snow guns on them, giving us a greater distribution. The snow crystals are airborne longer, so the snow is considerably dryer. We're also installing guns that oscillate. This helps to eliminate the piles that you get with stationary guns — you don't have to spend as much time and labor spreading it around.

At Boyne Mountain and Boyne Highlands we have 100% snowmaking on all skiable runs. When we cut out new slopes, we dig trenches and provide for underground air, water and electrical lines right along with tree removal and grading.

Providing snow when Mother Nature doesn't has its price. It costs millions in wells, holding ponds, pumps, electrical wire, pipes, snowmaking guns and other equipment. That's just the start. On a $3 million system, our raw cost for labor is $63 per hour and spiraling upward along with inflation. Sometimes you have as many as three shifts operating. System depreciation is $250 per hour. We calculate it averages about $600 an hour to make snow. In 24 hours that's $13,000. In the early season we run the guns around the clock, weather permitting, at both the Mountain and the Highlands. That's $26,000 per day in Michigan alone, $50,000 at four resorts. That's our cost.

Turning on the snowmakers like this in late October and early November is a crap shoot. At Boyne we almost always get some natural snow in those months. Daily, I sit at my desk, looking at short- and long-range forecasts from a national weather service, wondering when to call in the crews and have them crank up the guns. I also consult with our pilot, Bill McElroy, who studies weather for our mutual self-preservation.

What usually happens is that I take a gamble, ordering everybody to stand by to go into action whenever the temperature drops below freezing, regardless of the amount of snow on the ground before Christmas. Because I just know a thaw will come and ruin the holiday season. My only insurance is to build up enough of a base to outfox the thaw and the Man above.

With our snowmaking capacity and a few days a week of cold weather we can almost always open for the Thanksgiving weekend. Our skiing patrons depend on that. In 40 years we've disappointed them only once by failing to have at least two or three slopes open by then. I'm proud of that. I'm also proud that, in 1993, the readers of *Ski Magazine* rated Boyne Mountain #1 in Snowmaking in the United States. And Boyne Highlands was ranked #4.

I think that one of the reasons we earned these accolades is because we make snow many nights during the winter whenever temperatures are right, but not because we don't have enough base on the slopes (we usually get through March and have around 60 to 80 inches on the major runs at Boyne Mountain and Boyne Highlands). We make the extra snow to provide top-quality skiing for the next day, using giant tillers to fold the new stuff into the old, much like a cook folding egg whites in cake batter. Our state-of-the-art tillers and groomers are at work nearly every night during the season, virtually guaranteeing that ice-free conditions greet our skiers the next morning.

Western ski areas have long depended on natural snow. Some years when snowfall is light or late, it's caused bankruptcies. Boyne was among the first to install snowmaking in the West. We now have snowmaking equipment on a number of key runs at our Western ski areas – Big Sky and Brighton Ski Bowl – and we continue to add more each season. Vail, Aspen and most of the rest are now doing the same.

The Christmas-New Year's season of 1994-95 was one where Ullr, the Norse God of Chase and Skiing, had turned his back on the Midwest, but dumped tons of snow in parts of the West, particularly Utah, where nearly 200 inches had fallen in November alone.

Back home, temperatures were unseasonably warm, averaging 20 degrees higher than normal all through December, and the entire Midwest was bare of the white stuff as Christmas approached. And it was even warm at night, so we could only turn on our snow-guns for a few hours two or three times a week at most. By Christmas, and for the first time in my memory, the ground was bare.

Because we had started early making snow at both the Mountain and Highlands, stockpiling it whenever we could in November and December, we were in good shape, but our competitors were in disasterland. All of our ski runs had from three to four feet of "artificial" snow, and the skiing was very good. Our problem became one of convincing skiers who were still using their golf clubs that we really, truly, honestly had skiable snow.

I authorized my "silver bullet" — a reserve fund of dollars for use in an emergency. Our ad and marketing staff rushed through a "Guaranteed Skiing" campaign in Midwest newspapers and over radio and TV stations, sending out ad prints, photos and video tapes, taken daily, showing piles of snow and white-clad slopes amid brown fields. It worked — despite a front-page story in a major newspaper headlined in bold type **"Up north, no snow = no dough."** Our Christmas-New Years holiday season, which represents so much of our ski season business, was saved.

In many ways this lack of natural snow during the holidays proved to be a blessing in disguise; we didn't have to plow our streets, parking lots and airport runway, there were no roofs to clear or walks to shovel, no slippery spots to salt.

More importantly, it erased all doubts in the minds of thousands of skiers of the high-quality and reliability of Boyne's snowmaking. It converted the non-believers into believers. The word-of-mouth advertising that will be spread by those who came that Christmas season will pay off many times over. And maybe, just maybe, the media will become believers, too. But I'm not holding my breath.

If the big Man up there in the sky would only eliminate thaws, and bring us seasonal storms and cold weather as initially programmed in His original plan, all ski operators everywhere would be most thankful. Until then, and even after, let the snow guns roar.

Alpine racing has grown to become one of today's most popular winter sports. Races are attended by thousands and are heavily supported by TV and advertising dollars. It wasn't always this way. Most people don't know that Boyne not only participated in the first professional race in the United States in 1961, but was also the series originator. Kircher explains how it all started.

Circa 1960

Pro Racing

I had long wondered what would happen to amateur ski racers after competing in the Olympics and world championship races. I called Sepp Reusch, president of Stowe and head of the National Ski Association, and broached the subject of forming a professional ski racing tour. He flat out said it was a bad idea. The sport was for the recreational skier, not the professional. I then called Friedl Pfeiffer, who headed the ski school for the Aspen Ski Corporation. He liked the idea and became the driving force behind the racing tour, originally named the International Professional Skiers Association.

We each anted up $5,000 to get the thing started. Friedl invited me out to Aspen for the first pro race because we had contracted to hold the second race at the Mountain.

All the great skiers of the era showed up at the Boyne event, among them Stein Eriksen, Anderl Molterer, Ernst Hinderseer, Max Marolt, Christen Pravda, Les Streeter and, of course, Othmar Schneider.

Eriksen was the odds on favorite if the course was icy, as he was considered the world's best on ice. Molterer was favored if the snow was soft, which it turned out to be at race time. Each pro made four runs down a tough slalom course on Hemlock and the winner was the one with the fastest combined time for the four runs.

The surprise winner that year was the oldest racer in the field, Christian Pravda. Molterer was second and Hinderseer was third. Eriksen, who was coming off an Achilles heel injury, fell. Schneider also fell.

The race at the Mountain was the first one where racers put on a freestyle exhibition. They had been reluctant to do so because they thought that Eriksen would be an automatic winner because of his famous flip. When he agreed not to do his flip in the competition, the others fell in line. In this event, Othmar and Stein made amends for their falls in the races. Othmar won first place money in the freestyle with his stylish dash through the moguls and his finishing Royal Christi, and Stein came in second with his flowing style and exciting leaps off the moguls.

Boyne put up the purse for this first pro freestyle event and I remember that we charged spectators who hadn't bought a lift ticket $1.50 to watch. I was the president of the Central United States Ski Association (CUSSA) at the time. We donated the proceeds evenly between the pro racing association and CUSSA in support of junior racing. Jim McKay, the well known radio and TV sportscaster, handled the broadcast and it was aired nationally by ABC.

Boyne also participated in what was called the Team Ski Championships. Each ski resort would enter its top racers and top ski school people to compete against the participating area teams. One year our Boyne team won the World Championship. Aspen and Vail were there, too. In those days Aspen couldn't afford to field a team, so they hooked up with Vail and they called themselves the Colorado Team. I was proud of our victory. Our Boyne instructors were world champs!

Ski racing, professional and amateur, has grown immensely since those early days, and is a regular part of the TV sports fare. It's the most watched event in the Winter Olympics. Tens of thousands of skiers participate each year in the National Standards Amateur Racing program. Almost all ski clubs hold ski races for their members. At Boyne we annually sponsor an international professional ski race featuring the world's best skiers, and have developed special slopes for racing events that separate the racers from our recreational skiers.

I'm pleased to say that Boyne was instrumental in supporting the fledgling pro racing circuits and continues to play a major role in professional ski racing, as well as encouraging and sponsoring amateur racing.

John Bartley first became acquainted with Everett Kircher when Everett was still involved in the car business in Detroit. An avid skier and ski instructor, John and his wife Jane wanted to get into the ski business. Everett convinced them to build and own the lodge at Boyne Highlands. They did and it still stands today.

Through other eyes

John Bartley

I was operating a used car lot just outside of Detroit in the 1950s before I became involved with Boyne Mountain. Like other used car dealers, my product sources were the trade-ins taken by new car dealers. Kircher Motors on Detroit's east side was a Studebaker dealership, owned by Everett Kircher, one of the youngest car dealers in the state. I'd shop his lot regularly, looking for "cream puffs" to buy and resell.

Cream puffs were the lower-cost popular models – used Fords and Chevys in decent condition – and the easiest to resell. Nobody wanted the "dogs." They were the clunkers new dealers often had to take in on trade to make a sale. They were really tough for any-body to move. You'd be lucky to break even.

Used car guys like me wouldn't touch the dogs, and the new car dealers usually had to junk them. Keeping them around downgraded their lots, so they would get rid of them any way they could.

Kircher didn't like losing money, so he put his mind in fast-forward and came up with a brilliant scheme. No more buying just the cream puffs. He would only sell his trade-ins in lots of ten. He'd let you have three, sometimes four, cream puffs but you had to take three dogs and fill out the quota with some mid-range models. Otherwise, no deal.

We used car guys didn't like the allotment arrangement one bit. But the other new car dealers got wind of Kircher's policy and followed suit. Kircher had changed the whole trade-in spectrum overnight, and we used car dealers had to learn to live with it.

Later in life, my wife Jane and I, both certified instructors, were enamored with the sport and decided to get into the ski business ourselves. We'd gone to Vail and picked out a piece of property that would be fine for a motel. I called Everett, told him what we were planning to do, and asked him what he thought of the idea.

"Forget Vail," he said. "Boyne Highlands is going to boom and I'll let you in on the ground floor. I'll lease you the land and help you with the financing if you build a lodge here."

We built the three story, 70-room Bartley House next door to the main Highlands Inn and have never regretted it. Everett was right, Boyne Highlands did boom. I headed up the Boyne Mountain ski school for two years, and developed a great admiration for the man. He had an incredible ingenuity about what the skiing public needed and wanted and what the business required. If the learn-to-ski-weekers didn't know what skiing was all about when they came to Boyne, they did by the time they left.

Everett was years ahead of everyone when it came to developing and operating a ski resort and attracting the potential skiing public. I don't think the industry realizes what an important part he has played in the development of Alpine skiing in the United States. I think that when people learn more about what Everett has contributed to skiing, he will be remembered as one of the dedicated pioneers of the business.

Everett Kircher should be in every ski hall of fame for what he did for the ski industry in its infancy.

With the ski business profitably humming along, Kircher turned his attention to the challenge for summer revenue. The idea of a golf course on Boyne property was suggested and Kircher began his intense study of a second sport. In the ensuing 40 plus years since that initial venture into golf, Boyne has experienced incredible growth in the golf business. At present, Boyne Highlands' and Boyne Mountain's seven championship golf courses and Bay Harbor's glorious 27 holes help northern Michigan earn the prestigious reputation as America's Summer Capital of Golf.

And Then Came Golf

By the mid '50s, I was happy with how the ski business was going. Our ski weeks were averaging between 400 and 500 skiers during the week and 1,500 on weekends. Summer was another story. We'd managed to get an occasional convention or business meeting in between ski seasons, but most spring and summer months the majority of our rooms were empty. Tourists hardly ever stopped by, mostly because we were known strictly as a winter ski resort. And without business in the warmer months, I couldn't keep a staff employed year around except for a few maintenance people.

One spring day, I was standing at the bar in our lounge, staring out at brown weeds poking through the last of the season's snow, and wondered aloud how to increase summer occupancy. A friend, Bill Harbor, said, "Everett, you need a golf course. There aren't many courses up North, but a lot of golfers vacation here. A golf course would be a sure-fire attraction."

I liked the idea. It seemed to have some potential. And, in this case building a small golf course on property we already owned didn't appear to be risky. It might even be fun.

Although I had played a little golf, I knew about as much about golf course design as I did about nuclear physics. But Bill Harbor was a good player. He belonged to a private club downstate and he offered to help. With not much to lose, the two of us staked out a nine-hole Executive course in front of the lodge and off to the south. We used bamboo slalom poles to locate tees, greens and hazards wherever the available land seemed suitable. After the course layout was done, Bill Harbor left for home and I went to work.

I had an old bulldozer and an ancient Ford tractor with a terracing blade that my father had given me. I just started pushing dirt around, and wound up with one par 4 and eight par 3 holes. I also put in a sprinkling system that had to be operated manually. What a headache that turned out to be, trying to get people to turn on the right sprinkler at the right time. But people initially liked to play the course and still do. We redid the course in 1990, eliminating some of the original holes and adding new ones, including two new par 4s. It's a fun course, no pushover, even for the scratch golfer. Some of the par 3s are 180 to 200 yards so even the pros don't bring it to its knees when we have a special event there during Boyne's Tournament of Champions.

Not only did that little course give me some important experience in golf course design and construction, it got me really interested in the game. It also convinced me that if I wanted summer business to grow, golf was indeed one way to go.

I began playing a lot when the course was completed. I'll never forget the even par round

I shot there one day. I even captured it on 16 mm film, every single shot and putt. I couldn't do anything wrong. My only other claim to golfing fame came years later when I shot better than my age: a 75 at Boyne South in Naples, Florida, when I was 76. I followed it up a year later with a 76.

Golf interested me enough that I began studying it seriously. I bought a number of books on golf course design and instruction. Hole layout and the architect's strategy behind each I found fascinating. For example, Donald Ross used to design par four holes with a bunker placed 30 yards or so in front of a green to confuse players. Then they'd come up short with their second shot and have to chip close and sink a putt to make par. I discovered that Donald Ross courses weren't penal or heroic, they were strategic yet fair.

The first 18-hole championship course we built was at Boyne Highlands. I brought in Robert Trent Jones to design the course because he was the most famous golf architect at the time, and his name would create attention and publicity. He agreed to take on the project for $30,000, a lot of money back then, but one tenth of what he charged a few years later.

Jones routed out the course using topographic maps I provided. When we inspected the terrain on foot, some of the ground he had planned to use was blueberry marsh. Even though building over a marsh was possible (this was before the days of the Wetlands Act) it would take a mountain of fill and a carload of money.

My staff and I rerouted a number of holes. We used Jones' number one, rerouted and designed numbers two, three and four, and used Jones' five. For six, I found a little ridge next to the marsh that looked like a place the Flintstones would live, so we put in a par three that we called the Flintstone hole. We also rerouted and redesigned seven. All of the rest were Jones' holes.

An amusing thing happened one of the first times I played the course. I had teed up my ball on the Flintstone hole, waiting for the green to clear. A red squirrel was chattering noisily in a pine tree near the teeing area, as if we were invading his territory. Suddenly, he ran down the tree, grabbed my teed-up ball, then scampered back to his tree with my ball in his mouth. Even with coaxing, he refused to drop the ball. He kept up his chattering. At the base of the tree we found two other slightly chewed golf balls — he obviously hadn't just picked on us.

We had another ball thief on the dogleg second hole. Golfers had reported that their drive was missing after they had hit it just around the bend in the fairway. We finally found out that it was a fox who had taken a liking to balls. He'd grab them from the fairway and dart off into the adjacent swamp. One of the staff donned a pair of boots and checked out the swamp. He found nearly a bushel of golf balls in a pile, all with teeth marks. The fox finally left, probably tired of his brand of golf.

I named the course the Heather, continuing the Highlands' Scottish theme. The Heather was an instant winner. In 1971, it was ranked as one of Golf Digest's Top 100 courses, somewhat unusual for a relatively new golf course. By all accounts, the Heather started the golf boom in northwestern Michigan, America's Summer Golf Capital.

As the summer business grew and prospered, we added another 18 holes at Boyne Highlands. We blended it in with the Heather and wound up with the Heather and Moor courses. I mixed the two for economic reasons. Both courses started and ended at the existing clubhouse. There wouldn't be a need to build and staff a second pro shop.

In between building the Heather and Moor, we designed and built the Alpine course at Boyne Mountain. Years before I had bought a few hundred acres on the back side of the mountain on the advice of Chuck Moll. "What do we want it for?" I asked at the time. Chuck had no answer except that it was for sale, and it was cheap. Neither one of us envisioned a golf course on it. The purchase was a stroke of luck.

The Alpine opened in 1970 on that property and turned out to be a jewel. It takes a memorable mile-and-a-half scenic golf cart ride up the mountain from Deer Lake to get to the first tee. That ride in itself got a lot of favorable comments and press, and still does.

The course features great views as it swoops down to Deer Lake. It's challenging without being penal, so people come back to play it again and again. Fortunately, I learned early that you don't make a course too intimidating if you want repeat business. Rank and file golfers don't need the grief.

After the Moor course was completed at the Highlands, my son Stephen and I began planning and building the Monument course at the Mountain. We needed a second 18 there to handle convention business. I put my heart and soul into that project. Stephen and I were able to just let our imaginations run wild.

From the first tee to the final green we paid as much attention to irrigation, drainage and potential maintenance pitfalls as we did to the esthetics of design. With the cost of labor, course maintenance can gobble up profits faster than anything else. (I'm always amazed at the size of maintenance crews at some courses, particularly private ones. Everyone seems to have an assistant, and it takes three guys to fix a sprinkler head. It's a small wonder that dues and assessments are as high as they are. Most golf clubs could cut staff in half and maintain conditions just as well.)

The Monument turned out far better than Stephen and I had hoped. *Golf Digest* named it runner up for Best New Resort Course in the U.S. for 1987.

While the course was being built, I kept scribbling out possible names. One day the idea hit me. During construction, we unearthed gigantic boulders weighing several tons each. Rather than dump them in the woods, I decided to use them to designate the tee boxes and also use them as markers to identify the 150-yard fairway-to-green distances, (typically done with stakes or small bushes). One PGA individual said that the USGA and PGA might not like permanent 150-yard markers to identify distances. "Fine," I told him. "They're welcome to move them for their tournaments."

Taking the idea a step further, I decided it would be great to use the tee-box boulders to honor golfing legends – monuments to their golfing accomplishments for legions of golfers to see and remember.

I had my marketing staff contact the two winningest professional golfers of all time, Sam Snead and Kathy Whitworth. We flew them to Boyne, staged a big press party and invited the public to attend. Writers from most of the important golf publications came. The pair put on an exhibition for the public. They played the course, and each chose a hole to be named in their honor. We then had bronze plaques highlighting their individual achievements mounted on a boulder at the hole of their choice. Snead made the 18th — an island hole — his personal choice, calling it, "One of the most intimidating holes I've ever played."

That was the kickoff of a highly successful marketing program. We've followed it up year after year. Gene Sarazen, Paul Runyon, Byron Nelson and Peggy Kirk Bell are among other greats who have played the course and designated holes. Ultimately, we'll have 36 plaques. Two on each hole, one for men and one for women. And one of them is mine. After I was elected to the Michigan Golf Hall of Fame for my contributions to the game, I chose my favorite, a hole we had called the Nash hole because of an ancient Nash automobile we buried in the fairway. I surrounded its "grave" with sand, and wound up with an unusual hazard and a split fairway. I guess I'll always be a car salesman at heart.

When it came time for a third course at Boyne Highlands, I wanted it to be a Donald Ross type course. I had read books about him and visited courses he had designed. I admired his design philosophy where he created courses that were strategic, rather than what the golf course architects call heroic (long and tough) or penal (long, tough and miserable). He was the greatest golf course designer and most prolific architect who ever lived. Unquestionably, he was the "Father of Golf Course Architecture in America," being credited with the design of some 500 golf courses in this country.

What fascinated me about Ross was how much he did with so little. He didn't have any background in reading topographic maps, irrigation, engineering or landscaping. He was a golf pro who learned clubmaking and the game in Scotland at Royal Dornock and St. Andrews. When he came to America at the turn of the century he first worked as a pro at Pinehurst, North Carolina, where he began his design career. One of his most famous creations is Pinehurst No. 2, his favorite venue as well as a favorite of many of America's top players.

Ross didn't build courses where there were trees. He had no way to clear them. He didn't have modern earth moving equipment, yet his courses remain as some of the best in the world. He was a master at working with the land that he had. His contoured greens with undulating rolls became his most famous trademark.

Ross stated that golf "should be a pleasure, not a penance." That philosophy jelled perfectly with mine. Unfortunately, I couldn't hire him to lay out the course I wanted to build. He died in 1948. I figured if I couldn't get the man, maybe I could duplicate some of his best holes from his most famous courses.

That inspiration led to an odyssey of thousands of miles of travel and years of effort and plenty of misgivings for awhile, too. Son Stephen and I visited many Ross courses across the country, most of them listed by Golf Digest in their List of Top 100 rankings. It became an engineering job – selecting and fitting famous Ross holes into our existing terrain.

Noted PGA golf instructor Jim Flick, my son Stephen, and other Boyne golf pros assisted in the selection process. Our engineers traveled to the course sites to map distances, elevations, bunkers and hazards, paying particular attention to the green complexes that were Ross trademarks. We had to get permission from the courses, naturally, but they were all cooperative, many even loaning us the original hole blueprints.

Armed with grids of greens, the blueprints and key measurements, we began construction in 1985 and completed seeding in 1988. Three long years! The holes selected are duplicates of the original holes as they exist today, incorporating the modifications made by the clubs in recent years to keep pace with the modern game and its equipment.

All holes are not carbon-copy duplicates. You couldn't recapture every fairway roll and subtle contour. Certain holes do not have the landscaping of their copied counterparts. Surrounding terrain differs – a forest of northern hardwoods will never resemble a stand of tropical palmettos, for example. The yardages of most duplicated holes are identical, however, as are the elevations between tees and greens. Tee shot landing zones, bunkers and ponds have been sized and positioned to match their models. Special care was taken to reproduce the size, shape and subtleties of green complexes – distinctive Ross trademarks.

The extra effort put into the Ross course has, in hindsight, turned out to be worth the sweat and tribulations. Golfers can play holes from courses they otherwise could only read about – Scioto, Pinehurst #2, Oakland Hills, Inverness, Seminole, Bob O'Link, Aronimink, Wannamoisett and others of golfing lore. Members of the courses the holes were chosen from have visited and approved of the duplications. And the Donald Ross Society – a group of golfers who pay tribute to Ross and play his layouts – have held annual meetings at Boyne Highlands and praise the course. Stephen and I find that very gratifying.

As this book was being written, a fourth course at Boyne Highlands was under construction. It's a cooperative design by Arthur Hills, perhaps the leading architect around today, and my son Stephen. It's probably going to be the best of the earlier five courses.

Another recent development is our spectacular Bay Harbor resort in Petoskey. The site consists of nearly three miles of spectacular frontage on Lake Michigan, as dramatic and breathtaking a piece of land as the Monterey Peninsula where the Pebble Beach course is located. The 27 holes designed by Arthur Hills (in collaboration with Stephen), make it the most exciting golf project Boyne has ever attempted. When the holes and a new club-house are completed, Boyne will have more money invested in that project than all of our other courses.

As I mentioned earlier, I got interested in playing the game in my 40's and became a pretty decent golfer, shooting in the 80's. But Father Time and a couple of strokes took their inevitable toll on my golf game. My swing speed went from race to creep. Drives that used to soar out to about 230 yards began ending up at 150 yards with roll when I'd hit it on the sweet spot. On typical par four's, it became driver, three wood and a nine iron or wedge – even more on those gorilla par four's that golf architects love to design to frustrate 90% of all golfers.

Not only did this hurt my pride, it annoyed the hell out of me. Playing with certain friends, I'd be breaking my shoelaces on my second shots when some of them would be using short irons.

I also play a lot of golf with my wife, Lois, and with other couples our age. Lois is tiny, just over five foot, but very strong. Yet she only averages 135 yards on her drive. Most of the other wives hit it about the same distance, or less. And on many of the courses we play the ladies red tees are often just a few yards in front of the men's regular white markers. The women have a hell of a time reaching some par four's with three woods. The par five's are even worse.

For some reason, this doesn't seem to bother them too much. This is the way it is, always has been, so it must be right! So it's accepted.

Well, it's not my nature to accept things that I think aren't right. I play golf to enjoy it, not to get frustrated. So I began playing our Boyne courses from the women's tees instead of the men's. Chuck Moll, my right-hand man, resisted it when he played with me, but finally gave in, mostly to accommodate me. My sports announcer friend, Bill Flemming, with whom I play often, was horrified. "We can't do that! It's embarrassing! Degrading! "He finally capitulated, mainly because he's a fierce competitor, hates to lose, and no way was I going to have such a big advantage over him. But he still grumbles. While he doesn't admit it, I think he enjoys the shorter tees as much as I do.

Boyne bought a golf course in Naples, Florida. Our pro at the time, Rich Prange, hit his drive about 270 yards or longer. He didn't raise an eyebrow when I began playing from the women's red markers. But then I started playing in front of the reds at varying spots on the fairway, depending on the length of the holes. After a few rounds experimenting with various locations, I staked out what I'd decided upon and informed Rich that I wanted dirt brought in and new tee boxes built, as indicated. He was about as enthusiastic as a guy facing an IRS audit. But he came around and these forward tees got built, and now I can shoot my age.

At Boyne South we now have four tee boxes on most holes, designated not by sex but by color—blue, white, red and yellow. No men's. No women's. It's take your choice: Mr. or Ms. Golfer, bite off what pleases you. Our first five courses at Boyne Mountain and Boyne Highlands average five tee boxes on each hole. The new Arthur Hills course has at least five tees and some even have six.

Talk about violent reactions. When Boyne South first displayed these new tees, you'd think I'd trashed tradition – betrayed the sacred Royal and Ancient. Bastardized the game.

All reactions weren't negative, however. Some women began to play the yellows, and beat their husbands for the first time. Not all the men enjoyed this, of course. It damaged their macho egos. More and more, both sexes began to play the shorter tees, especially the senior seniors, like me. Some play them when there aren't too many people around, when they think nobody's looking, but few brag about it to their friends.

Like anything new, it will take time before such short tees are accepted. Most die-hards will never accept them. However, Golfweek Magazine published an article advocating short tees, citing studies that showed that most courses are much, much too long for the vast majority of golfers. They advocated additional tees with distances much like those of my forward tees at Boyne South. I consider that a vindication. Maybe it's a route to lots more fun for more golfers, male and female. Don't be surprised if you see a number of new courses adding short forward tees as an option for men and women.

My son Stephen talked me into something that I had many reservations about from the beginning. He'd been out to California and had seen a distance measuring system named Yardmark. It was an early prototype that used domino sized chips buried along the fairways that gave you yardage from wherever you stopped your golf cart — how far you hit your drive from the tee, how far to a particular hazard on a hole, how far to the green and how far to the pin position for the day. Receivers with computer chips mounted on golf carts showed these various yardages on screens. This initial system was supposed to be accurate to about a yard, but it wasn't always reliable as I found out later.

The young man who developed it, with the help of some engineers and physicists, then redesigned the system, using cross-reference radio signals from towers instead of chips buried in the ground. I had plenty of misgivings, but after many meetings and a promise of exclusive use in our region for a limited time, I let myself be talked into it. The original outlay was $400,000. The arguments Stephen used to sell me on it were: One, it would speed up play because golfers wouldn't have to wander around trying to located distances on sprinkler heads or pace off yards from yardage books; two, we could increase greens fee a few dollars a round on the course where we installed the system, eventually permitting us to recover our investment; three, it would be an innovation that would get us a bundle of publicity in the golf publications and attract new customers,and reason number four, we could use it year round, at Boyne Highlands in the spring and summer months and at Boyne South in the winter months.

We had all sorts of problems with the system at first, mostly with programming and visibility. The screens on the devices were small and difficult to read, especially when the sun created a glare. The screen backgrounds were green in color and the letters showing the distances were black—a bad design at best. What irritated me the most was that the yardage from the tee telling you how far you had hit your drive flashed on the screen for only a few seconds, then flipped over to the other distance information. There were all sorts of numbers on the screen. Before I could get focused on the length of my drive, that figure would disappear and the other yardage would pop up.

Finding out how far my drive traveled was the only measurement that really interested me. It's one of the main reasons I had agreed to the purchase. How far it is to the pin is secondary in my case. On most par four holes I know I don't have a club in my bag that can reach the green with my second shot if I hit it perfectly. After that second shot, I'm usually close enough to judge the distance that's left to the green or pin just by eyeballing.

I'm still convinced that the length of the drive is the measurement that the average golfer wants the most. Then when he finds out, nine times out of ten, he's in for a rude awakening. Everybody thinks they hit it farther than they actually do. I've met guys who believe they average 250 yards off the tee, but the Yardmark screen says 205.In effect, it tells him he's a fabricator, and he's not a bit happy with that revelation.

The early problems with the system have recently been resolved. Now, the screen is much larger and the words are printed in black on a white background. Instead of relying on radio signals from towers, the signals are transmitted by the G.P.S. satellite system and distances are accurate to within a foot. All of the data shows up on the screen and stays visible, changing only when you move the cart.

I never envisioned golf as a profit center for Boyne – rather as a necessity to keep our winter people employed and to attract meeting and convention people. It can't compare to skiing. On our eight golf courses in Michigan, you can only run 200 players through a single course in a day, for a total of 1,600. Our greens fee rates vary from $65 to $99, depending on the season and the course. With all of the employee play, pros, special golf package deals and freebies, we average about $60 per round. That adds up to $72,000 on a crowded weekend day. Our lift ticket rates in 1995 averaged $35. On good weekends we can ski 12,000 a day in Michigan at the two resorts. It doesn't take a math major to see why I tell people that Boyne is in the ski lift ticket business, not the golf business.

But this sure is a fun summer job.

JimFlick first became acquainted with Everett Kircher when he came to Boyne as part of Golf Digest's touring ski school. Jim became a friend and admirer, and has since brought his Jack Nickalaus/Jim Flick golf instruction to Boyne and is currently setting up a Jim Flick golf school at Bay Harbor.

Through other eyes

Jim Flick

Everett Kircher, "Mr. K." as I prefer to call him, is well known in the world of skiing for the many contributions he has made to the sport — a true visionary in every sense of the word. But too few know that he's been a visionary where the game of golf is concerned.

I first became acquainted with Mr. K. when Bob Toski and I came to Boyne to teach in one of our *Golf Digest Golf Instruction Schools* in 1976. He was more than an on-looker. He was like a sponge, soaking up all of the knowledge he could about the swing. And in our second year, both he and his wife, Lois, attended our school as students. I've done more golf schools than anybody, but I've never met anybody whose mind is more inquisitive and more thirsting for information about golf than his.

Mr. K. was the first one to bring Robert Trent Jones, the world-famous golf architect, to design a resort golf course in northern Michigan, and, in fact, had a hand in routing a few holes himself. The course, named the Heather, quickly became one of *Golf Digest's Top 100 U.S. Courses.*

The Heather triggered a golf course explosion in northern Michigan, including more courses at Boyne Mountain and Boyne Highlands, and more than forty in what is now called "America's Summer Golf Capital," creating golf courses and tourism employment for thousands.

Mr. K. was the first person who was not afraid to have the first tee located quite a distance away from the clubhouse. That took a pretty strong individual, because up until that time most every golf course started with the first tee and the tenth tee adjacent to the clubhouse. His Alpine and Monument courses at Boyne Mountain require a mile-long cart ride up a scenic trail to reach the first tees at the top of the ski mountain, with the courses playing down to the eighteenth holes at the clubhouse. Once considered a no-no, this innovation is not considered unusual in the industry now. No longer must you have the first and tenth tees and the ninth and eighteenth greens starting and finishing at the pro shop or clubhouse.

Another of Mr. K.'s innovations is the contouring of the bunkers on Boyne's courses. Rather than just having a sand-filled pit where the ball rolls down to the bottom, providing a relatively easy lie, the larger bunkers may have two or three contoured "humps" that often require a variety of more difficult sidehill and downhill shots.

He's also been at the forefront in making his courses more enjoyable and playable for older golfers who, because of age or diminished physical skills, simply don't have the length to reach greens in two or three shots when playing from normal tee boxes. After observing that the average male golfer seldom exceeds 225 yards on his drive, and the average female golfer has difficulty hitting her drive more than 150 yards, Mr. K. has built forward tees on his courses where average players have a chance to reach greens in a regulation number of strokes. Subsequently, the Boyne courses are more enjoyable and less frustrating for many golfers to play.

Golf is a difficult game to learn to play well, arguably the most difficult of all sports. It's the only game where the practice facility where you train is different than one where you play. A lot of people have built golf facilities where the practice ranges are an afterthought and are often located considerable distances from the clubhouse or pro shop. Mr. K. has not let that happen. The practice ranges at the Boyne are world-class facilities with huge expanses of grass in the teeing areas. You don't have to practice your iron shots on gouged up turf that's down to the dirt like you find at driving ranges and practice areas at many golf courses. He's also built an outstanding learning and practice facility at Boyne Highlands where we hold Nicklaus/Flick golf instruction schools each year.

When I watch the game of golf, I see people who want to progress without going through the embarrassments that are a part of the game. No matter who you are, you're going to have failures and embarrassments. To improve you have to accept them, learn from them and put them behind you. That takes a lot of determination and spirit. It's especially true in Mr. K.'s case. He's physically challenged because of a couple of strokes he's had, making it difficult for him to maintain balance. That kind of handicap would stop most people, but it hasn't stopped Mr. K. It only seems to make him stronger and more determined. He's built up the heel on his golf shoe to compensate somewhat, and he gets out there on the practice range and golf course and not only ignores the handicap but beats it. To me, it's a lot of fun to watch him play and practice with that inner drive and determination.

Everett Kircher has a thirst for knowledge that is second to none of anybody I have ever known in my life. His tremendous drive and in depth understanding of how things work and what makes them work is a key to his many successes in golf, in skiing and in life.

Kircher's recipe for success includes immersing himself in the study of that particular subject. For example, although he was constantly told he could not 'make' snow, he studied and practiced the mixture of cold air and water until he succeeded. He is driven to win by overcoming any obstacle with the power of knowledge. Here, he relays his hunting experiences and his expertise of the sport.

In the Hunt

My Uncle Will taught me to fish. His brother Frank was the one who introduced me to hunting. Uncle Frank would get me up at dawn to go squirrel hunting with a .22 rifle. Later in the afternoon, Uncle Will would put a fishing rod in my hands, grab a can of bait and we'd be off to the Big Piney to see what was biting. Sounds exhausting now, but not back then when I was twelve years old and full of energy. I was a city kid and this was big stuff. I didn't want to miss a day doing either, and my uncles seemed to get a real kick out of teaching me.

Squirrels were about the only game I got a chance to hunt back in the 1920s in Blooming Rose, Missouri. The deer and turkey populations had been hunted out. Long seasons with few restrictions had killed them off.

We always took a dog along on squirrel hunts. He'd smell out the critters and tree them. And it usually took two of us to have a successful hunt. Once a squirrel spotted you, he'd run to the opposite side of the tree to hide. So you had to have a person on each side. If you were hunting alone the squirrels would just keep circling with you and you wouldn't get a shot.

Uncle Frank, gave me my first rifle, a single-shot Winchester .22. I shot quite a few squirrels on my visits to Blooming Rose and learned a bit about biology by skinning and cleaning them. I had my share of squirrel stew, watching how my aunt seasoned and cooked it, storing this tidbit of cookery away for future use.

Later my uncle gave me a prized 20-gauge shotgun that I used for years hunting ducks, pheasants and partridge. I bought guns for my sons, John and Stephen, when they were old enough to hunt. And I taught them gun safety as my uncle had done with me. Fortunately, we've never had a firearms accident in the family because of that early training.

John Norton, one of my original partners in the Boyne Mountain Ski Club, asked me, "Why don't you try hunting with a bow?" It sounded like something different, so I borrowed a bow and a couple of arrows from him and we went tramping through the woods at the Allegan State Forest, looking for deer.

That hunt wasn't successful, even though there were plenty of deer there. You can't expect to get a shot with a bow by wandering around in the woods. You have to be still and hidden in a blind, and downwind so the deer can't smell you. But I got interested in bow hunting and wanted to try again.

John took me to a small archery tackle shop on Twelfth Street in Detroit, owned by a tall, wiry man – Fred Bear. Fred showed me one of the bows he used and asked me to pull it. It was a 72-pound longbow, the bow used before the recurve bow came along, and long before the compound bow (with all the strings and pulleys) was invented.

I couldn't get the bow back a foot. He could draw it back all the way and hold it, seemingly without effort. And he could do the same with an 80-pound bow he showed me. Finally, he equipped me with a bow I could handle, and that first year I killed a deer with it. I became hooked on bow hunting.

Fred Bear became famous for bagging lions, tigers, elephants, grizzlies, polar bears – anything that walked or crawled – with a bow and arrow. He built Bear Archery Company, sold it and retired a millionaire.

Hunting has taken me to many places – Africa, Mexico, Canada, Austria, Norway and, of course, throughout the United States – for many species of game. I've hunted ducks and geese in Michigan, Indiana, Chesapeake Bay and in the far reaches of northern Ontario.

I've been to Africa three times, shooting an elephant, cape buffalo, leopard and sable. The sable is a beautiful animal. All black in color with a black mane, pretty head and long, swept-back antlers. The leopard almost got me before I got it. The animal had been driven into a thicket. I stumbled as it charged, and was fortunate to get a shot off before it got me.

I've hunted successfully in Montana, once getting a bighorn sheep after climbing for hours up a steep mountain. The ram was above me on an overhanging cliff and over 200 yards away, almost straight up. He fell just a few yards from where I was sitting.

In Wyoming, with my bow, I have bagged elk and mule deer. Many of the animals I've shot are of trophy caliber. I've had them mounted and they are now displayed on a wall in the main dining room at Boyne Highlands along with others shot by my son John.

A few years back in Montana I shot and recovered an elk with a bow. I'm about through now with hunting deer with a bow. Just too many wounded and unrecovered carcasses.

If I had my way, the DNR would limit the deer to bucks only and shorten the season. No more than a week, or maybe ten days at most, for rifle, bow and musket, with a special season if the deer become too plentiful. This won't wash, politically. The farmers would scream about crops being ruined. A long deer season means big business for motels, party stores, ammo shops, gas stations and all sorts of businesses that rely on hunter income. They would put up such a howl that the politicians would run for cover. I've given up suggesting such a preposterous idea because it will never fly.

In Michigan, the waterfowl population is no longer in danger, unlike the deer. Thanks in a large part to Ducks Unlimited and other organizations, hundreds of thousands of acres of breeding grounds for ducks and geese have been purchased or leased from the Canadian government, and there have been strict bag limits imposed in many states.

I've been an avid duck and goose hunter for years, including a number of trips up north to Hudson Bay, near the remote town of Moosonee. It's an experience one can't forget. The Cree Indians are your guides, and can speak only broken English. But they can call geese like you can't believe, using their voices instead of artificial callers. I've seen them turn around a flock two miles distant that were heading in a different direction, bringing them right down to your decoys.

Starting in August, geese from the nesting grounds far to the north fly into rest and feed on the tundra grasses before again heading south. They come in flights so large that they nearly block out the sun.

Millions of ducks arrive, too, rafting in the Arctic and feeding in the tundra's ponds. It's a hunter's paradise. You're allowed five geese a day, but can only take five home. Your guide cleans and packs them, keeping the rest for his family. There's no hunting limit for the Indians.

As is apparent, hunting has been a big part of my life, much of it shared with the family, including my father in years past whom I taught to hunt. I hope to be physically able to hunt for a few more years before packing it in.

Kircher long had a dream to expand his operations to include a ski resort in the western United States. He pursued this dream vigorously, investigating Sun Valley in Idaho, Telluride in Colorado and a few others. Finally, in 1976, Kircher had an opportunity to buy the Big Sky Resort in Montana from well known television news anchor Chet Huntley. The subsequent purchase of Big Sky presented major challenges but also has turned out to represent a wonderful investment and success story.

Heading West

Horace Greeley didn't have me in mind when he exhorted his readers to "Go West young man, go West." But the insanely cheap jet airfares of the 1960s signaled an end to the continuing rapid expansion of the Boyne Mountain and Boyne Highlands skiing growth. I had watched my "regulars" plan week, even weekend, trips to the Rockies, especially in the March and April months. A jet ticket to Denver was well within the pocketbook of most. And what skier can resist the lure of the mountains? Certainly not me. I had taken a ski trip to the West or to Europe at least once a year since 1938.

The itch to own a ski resort in the West was a dream of mine and pestered me constantly. I began checking out possible Western acquisitions whenever I'd hear that one might be for sale. Many times I'd be contacted by owners who wanted to sell. In the late sixties, I found out that Sun Valley was on the market. The Union Pacific had decided to get out of the ski business. (The railroads were having their own battles with the airlines fighting for passengers.) The possibility of buying it was exhilarating, keeping me awake for weeks. Of all of the ski resorts in America, Sun Valley was my absolute favorite. I had skied it 13 years in a row, beginning in 1938, when the ski slopes were confined to Proctor and Half Dollar Mountains, before Bald Mountain was developed.

Sun Valley had everything. It was famous around the world. A movie had been made there with Sonja Heine, the darling of figure skating, an Olympic champion and movie queen. It was titled "Sun Valley Serenade," and the theme song of the movie "It happened in Sun Valley" was constantly played over the radio and became a big hit. John Payne, a former member of Glenn Miller's band, had the male lead. The movie was a hit, of course a love story in a romantic setting. It helped popularize the resort and winter fun.

"Baldy" itself was about as perfect a ski mountain as you could find, then or now. Nearly 3,500 feet of vertical, with bowls, bumps, long uninterrupted runs. In 1994 Skiing Magazine called it "The best cruising mountain on the planet." One of the things I liked most about it was the fact that its altitude at the summit was just slightly over 9,000 feet. You could breathe at that altitude even on the first day of your visit, unlike many of the ski mountains in Colorado. Lots of them are 12,000 feet or higher. Takes your body days to get acclimated unless you're a highlander. You can't make three turns without gasping for air. (Pilots know the danger. If you're flying an unpressurized plane, you're supposed to use oxygen at 10,000 feet.)

I also liked the town of Ketchem. A perfect ski town, not overly developed. About the only drawback was Sun Valley's location. Very difficult to get to even by car from Boise,

Twin Falls or Salt Lake City, the closest cities serviced by major airlines. There wasn't then, or isn't now, any way to avoid a harrowing drive on mountain roads. But skiers by the tens of thousands gladly suffer the inconvenience and road conditions to enjoy a skiing vacation there.

I will always regret not buying Sun Valley. But it was not to be. The price was in the neighborhood of $10 million. At the time money was the major deterrent. I was committed to substantial investments in Boyne Mountain and Boyne Highlands and couldn't bring myself to take on a major investment with a big debt load.

Later, Telluride in Colorado, came on the market. The asking price was about 2.5 million dollars, a reasonable price when compared to Sun Valley's asking price. I went with my family and some staff people to check it out. My sons, Steve and John, were about 10 and 15 years old, respectively, and very good skiers even then. They weren't too impressed with the mountain. Most of the runs then were on the advanced or expert side. And again, it wasn't skier friendly in terms of altitude; a typical 12,000-foot Colorado summit and nearly 9,000 feet at the base. I felt that the mountain didn't have enough intermediate skiing, being geared more to the expert skiers. The town was like many in Colorado's mountains, and to my way of thinking, nothing special.

I was wrong there. I'll never underestimate the power of a town again. The townsfolk pulled together and put the town and ski area on the map, despite the rather remote location and rugged terrain.

When we returned to Boyne, the family discussed the possible purchase. We took a vote, and Telluride lost. Upon reflection, we lost, too. At the asking price, Telluride would have been a steal. It's now a very popular and profitable ski area, growing in popularity every year.

At the time Telluride was up for grabs, an opportunity to buy a 50-50 interest in the Jackson Hole, Wyoming, ski area came up. I could have bought a half interest for $1.5 million, still a lot of money. But I never have liked partnerships, particularly equal partnerships with equal say. That always spells trouble, big time, down the line, and I have avoided those types of deals like I avoid a nest of hornets.

We also visited Copper Mountain and Keystone in Colorado, both of which were seeking reasonable offers. After checking them out, I declined to make a bid because the areas often suffered from a lack of snow, particularly in the early season. The first thing that would have to be done would be to install a large scale snowmaking system at either area – a costly undertaking I didn't want to consider.

In 1976, I was contacted to see if I had any interest in buying Big Sky, the Montana ski area started by former newsman Chet Huntley. He had retired from the Huntley-Brinkley newscast to pursue his dream, a resort in the Big Sky Country of Montana. Huntley was a Big Sky figurehead, a front man whose reputation was an asset. Chrysler Realty was the biggest stockholder, owning 55% of the stock. The rest was owned in varying proportions by Montana Power and Light, Burlington Railroad, Montsano Chemical, General Electric and Northwest Airlines. Huntley's share was minute.

The resort had lost over twenty million dollars in its last three years of operation and Chrysler, particularly, was eager to sell. In my mind, however, Big Sky had all of the ingredients of Sun Valley. I had visions of sugar-plums dancing in my head at the thought of owning "my own Sun Valley."

The first thing you see when approaching Big Sky from Bozeman, some forty miles from Big Sky, is Lone Mountain, a pyramidal peak that towers above the surrounding areas. It's awe-inspiring, reminding you of the Matterhorn on the Swiss-Italian border. It had magnificent terrain for skiers of all abilities, with seemingly endless room for more runs plus a virtually untapped bowl area at the top third of Lone Mountain.

The adjoining mountain and part of the resort was also terrific terrain and offered lots of room for ski run expansion. The base hub was the Huntley Lodge, a quality inn with 200 guest rooms, a few meeting rooms, dining room, cafeteria, shops and lounges. It was located slopeside with ski-in-ski-out convenience always a big plus.

All told, the property consisted of about 10,000 acres with nearly 4,000 still available for real estate development. There wasn't an altitude problem because the summit didn't exceed 10,000 feet. Annual snowfall averaged over 400 inches. Most importantly, the area was privately owned and need not come under the bureaucratic thumb of the U.S. Forest Service. You wouldn't have to go through years of negotiation to cut a tree or add a chairlift.

The huge losses the resort had suffered bothered me. But a quick tour of the facilities and offices helped explain why. Every secretary had a secretary. Staff stumbled over staff everywhere. It was a typical big corporation operation, much like General Motors and other huge companies in the late 1980s before they came to their senses and started wielding the downsizing ax.

I had little doubt that the Big Sky business could be turned around over time. It would take a large infusion of cash and a lot of planning and work. But the potential was there. I could envision Big Sky as a popular destination for the jet set and for Midwestern skiers, particularly those who skied at Boyne. With additional meeting and convention facilities the opportunity existed for substantial summer business which would be critical to success. The 18-hole Arnold Palmer golf course, while drastically in need of conditioning improvements, would help to attract conventions and other groups.

Believing that Boyne and other Midwestern skiers would go to Big Sky on their annual western pilgrimages was a huge miscalculation. They totally ignored it. They continued habitually to go to Aspen, Vail or some other Colorado ski resort. It took 10 years to get our season pass holders to make the trip and they didn't give Big Sky a try until we gave them free skiing as a season pass perk. Thank God for skiers from Florida, Georgia and Texas. Without them Big Sky would have gone broke.

Just outside the Big Sky gate was some of the best trout fishing and white-water rafting in the country. Even more exciting was the proximity of Yellowstone, the most popular national park in the country and just 18 miles from Big Sky's front entrance. With the right advertising and promotion we could profit from room nights all seasons of the year.

The family fell in love with the area right off the bat. We went home and took a vote. The decision was unanimous. We'd buy if the price was right. John Clark, our corporate attorney, did much of the negotiating for the purchase at the Chrysler Realty offices in Detroit. Some $56 million had been sunk into the development of Big Sky. We bought it for $10 million.

Lone Mountain Ranch was located on the Big Sky property, but was not included in the original purchase. It was a privately owned dude ranch that I could have bought for $150,000. The family wanted me to, and I shot myself in the foot for not listening to them. I loved horses, and so did my wife and both daughters. We had horses and a stable for many years at our Boyne Falls home and would ride regularly. The main drawback to the purchase was that I'd be so busy getting Big Sky off of the ground that I wouldn't be able to supervise the ranch operation and the proper care of the horses. And frankly, I didn't trust the ranch's employees to handle the operation without supervision.

Taking on the Big Sky operation was a bigger job than I had envisioned. We had to staff it with our own people and gradually eliminate the excess personnel on the payroll a necessary task that didn't endear me or Boyne people to the locals. Most of the employees that had to be let go were the real estate people that Chrysler had hired and a large marketing staff we couldn't use.

Within a few years I put my oldest son, John, in charge of the entire Big Sky operation. He was only 25 at the time, and plenty green. But he was a quick study in most matters and knew the ski business quite well, having been around it all of his life. Chuck Moll and I were in daily contact with him. Within three years we had added two new chairlifts, enlarged the Huntley Lodge dining room, developed new runs and began marketing residential lots – a long, slow process as it turned out.

We built a $20 million condominium hotel and convention center which quadrupled our summer activities. The whole project was a success because not only did we sell it out, but we also would receive 50 percent of the rentals. The owners are happy and so are we. The convention facilities include a 10,000 square foot convention hall, large theater and lecture hall.

Since then we have built 2 detachable lifts, high speed quads and a tramway to the top which gave us the country's largest vertical drop—4,150 vertical feet.

Not all of the expansion was done with ease, though. When we took over Big Sky there were about 200 condominium rooms built and sold by Chrysler Realty. The owner's association hired attorneys about two months before the statute of limitations ran out on whether you could sue if you didn't like your condominium and these ambulance chasers were around watching for that date.

They came in and started stirring up all this trouble. Are you satisfied with your condominium? Have you ever seen anyone who was satisfied with his condominium? They hired engineers (who were worse than the ambulance chasers) who wrote up a list of things that could have been done better. Chrysler Realty was forced to put $2 or $3 million into unnecessary repairs on the buildings.

We in turn, were sued along with Chrysler because we had bought Chrysler's stock. The Deer Lodge owners association was claiming millions of dollars of damage to their buildings beyond what was already repaired. It cost Chrysler $7 million to satisfy the lawsuit, we lost $2 million worth of condominiums.

Deer Lodge was condemned and we lost lift tickets from the 200 condominium owners for about 3 or 4 years. It was a huge impact on Big Sky at that time.

Buying Big Sky was our first expansion in the west, and was well worth the wait. It's truly a resort I'm proud to have in the Boyne family.

The Hemlock tree that gave Boyne Mountain's famous ski run its name.

Vandals cut away at it and destroyed it, so our workers
had to cut it down.

Hockey great Gordie Howe, oversees the tightening of
his son's skates at Boyne's early skating rink.

Kircher just lands one.

Kircher dedicates his own hole #16 at the Monument Course.

Life long friend Bill Fleming of ABC Sports fame.

Lone Peak Mountain towers above
Big Sky's mountain village

Even before micro-breweries were popular, there was
Boyne beer. This bottle features two famous skiers Stein
Eriksen and Kircher.

Big Sky, Montana.

Boyne South
golf course in
Naples, Florida.

A familiar picture of Steve and Everett Kircher recently
used for Boyne promotions.

Jim Flick instructs Everett and others at a Boyne special
event circa 1990.

Donald Ross, the legendary
course designer and inspiration for
18 holes at Boyne Highlands.

Byron Nelson chose the #1 hole on the
Monument Course for his namesake.

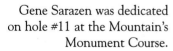

Gene Sarazen was dedicated
on hole #11 at the Mountain's
Monument Course.

Jim Flick, the world famous golf instructor and friend of
Boyne for over 25 years.

Kircher found another love early in his life – airplanes. Growing up across the street from an aircraft builder in Detroit piqued his interest in being able to fly. Although flight lessons were too expensive when he was young, he never let go of this dream and eventually became a pilot. Here he discusses the airplanes Boyne USA has operated, which truly eased travel between Boyne Mountain and their western operations.

Airborne

Flying airplanes interested me from the time I was very young, about eight years old. Right across the street from our house was this little building that looked like a two- or three-car garage. It was an airplane factory where they were building the first Stinson aircraft – little single-engine two-seaters. I watched them roll out the planes without the wings attached, and truck them to Detroit City Airport where they would be reassembled and flight-tested.

It was at that airport that I had my first flying experience. A sightseeing flight service took me up in a single-engine bi-plane with a joy stick control. I think the ride cost me five dollars for a half-hour. It was pretty exciting flying a few thousand feet above the city. I was intrigued and decided I wanted to learn to fly.

Being sixteen I was old enough, but I had to go for a physical first. I went to a doctor and he gave me a thorough going over. I passed it and got an okay on what I now know was a depth perception test. He had me pull strings attached to a little pillbox to line up two blocks. Armed with the exam papers I went back to the airport, signed up with an instructor and took a lesson. I was hooked! Unfortunately, that one lesson was all I could financially handle at the time, so I had to forget flying for a few years.

Shortly after I started Boyne, I met John Brennan. He was a retired Air Force officer and a skier. We palled around together in Detroit and at Boyne and he convinced me that I really ought to learn to fly, and that I should buy an airplane. Planes were not too expensive at the time, so I bought a four-seated Stinson and hangered it at Wayne Major Airport where most of the private flying was going on.

John taught me quite a bit about flying, map reading, navigation and radio, aeronautical principles, cross-country, night flying and other things a pilot has to know. I also took private lessons.

My first real flying adventure with the Stinson was a trip I made to Sun Valley. I'd had some cross-country experience, but nothing close to a Michigan to Idaho hop. I got the needed maps, planned my stops and took off. The Stinson was under-powered, capable of 90 to 100 miles per hour at a few thousand feet of altitude. I made a few quick stops for gas and flew to Hastings, Nebraska, where I visited a girl I knew, then headed for Sun Valley.

I remember I was at 12,000 feet over the mountains north of Salt Lake City, and getting low on gas. I had been bucking 60 mile-per-hour headwinds, making about 30 ground miles per hour. Although I had plotted my gas stops carefully, leaving plenty in reserve between flights, I hadn't anticipated the headwinds. I barely made it to Hailey, Idaho, where there was a small airstrip and fuel pumps.

The return trip from Sun Valley was great. I flew it all the way to Hastings, Nebraska, non-stop. I'd picked up a big, old tailwind at 10,000 feet and just sailed along, probably moving at about 200 mph.

My second airplane was a Helio Courier. It had huge wings and would take off and land at about 35-38 mph. Years later, after he got his license, son John flew it to Big Sky, Montana, where we sold it. Unfortunately, the person who purchased it crashed it on his first flight. There was a faulty wiring problem that a mechanic caused when he had worked on the plane. The cockpit filled with smoke and the pilot had to land in an irrigation ditch. He totaled the airplane, but fortunately was not badly injured.

The next Boyne plane was a Grumman Mallard — a big, twin-engine amphibian. By then we had hired Bob Nichols as our corporate pilot. Bob's personal plane was a single-engine float plane, so he had quite a bit of experience with water landings and takeoffs. We bought the Mallard from Christian Dior, the famous French clothes designer, and I sent Bob to France to pick up the plane. He flew it back, stopping to refuel in Scotland, Iceland, Greenland and Labrador.

Only 50 Mallards were ever built. They were sturdy brutes. While I was happy to get the Mallard, it had the ugliest paint job I ever saw on an airplane. It was purple and green with a black striping along the sides. If Dior designed clothes in colors like that he wouldn't have been able to sell a dress.

We took the Mallard on a number of trips, including a couple to Sun Valley. I was co-pilot, Nichols the captain. We took turns taking off and landing. A friend of mine who owned an advertising agency had one of his artists come up with a slick new paint design for the aircraft. We had the plane repainted a handsome combination of white, blue and red — Boyne Mountain colors. We also equipped it with new, turboprop engines, increasing its speed considerably.

I hated to part with the Mallard but I had the hots for a corporate jet. Affording one was another matter. New ones cost over two million dollars – too rich for my blood.

We heard that a company in Traverse City – B&B Aviation – was looking for a partner in their six-passenger Jet Commander. After a bit of negotiation we traded the Mallard for half interest in the jet and for a pressurized, 8-passenger Piper Navajo. B&B sold the Mallard to a Canadian airline a short time later and I had my jet.

FAA rules mandated that the Aero Commander required two licensed pilots with jet credentials, meaning I had to have an additional pilot. I added Bill McElroy to our staff. Bill was a retired Air Force and Air Force Reserve officer with over 30 years' experience in jets. On flights he was the captain and Bob Nichols was co-pilot. I sat in the right-hand seat on most flights, however, to get some experience in handling a jet-propelled aircraft. Actually, I found that flying a jet was no more difficult or complicated than flying a twin-engine propeller plane. Just more gadgets to learn.

We'd owned the Commander and Navajo for about two years when the Cessna company contacted us about a Citation I aircraft they had for sale. It was a demo plane, but had logged only 250 hours of flight time. This was a six-passenger-single-pilot craft that could fly rings around the Jet Commander. It was much faster and more fuel efficient. Having just bought Big Sky, it was exactly what I needed for the many trips I would have to make out to Montana. An additional plus was that it only required a single pilot, and I could act as co-pilot. I traded in the Navajo and Jet Commander and we bought the Citation I.

I was happy with the plane and we kept it for about two years. Cessna contacted me and said they'd make me a sweet deal on a Cessna Citation II, which was faster and larger than the Citation I. It could carry eight, plus pilots. The plane had been ordered by the Coast Guard, but they had canceled the order because of lack of funds. I was hesitant at first until Cessna told me that the plane was gutted out and I could choose the seating arrangements, upholstery and certain instrumentation. That did it. We traded in the Citation I and bought the II.

I was invited to see the prototype of the Cessna III at Callaway Gardens, a golf resort in Georgia. It would take three years before they would be able to deliver the first plane, and only twenty five would be produced. The "early in" buyers would get the opportunity to buy a III.

Golfing legend Arnold Palmer was number one on the list. Boyne was number eighteen. We put down a large deposit and by the time the plane was available we had it paid off. Then reality and my German tight-fistedness set in. That was a whale of a lot of money. My Citation II was perfectly fine. Saving an hour or so on trips to Big Sky wasn't worth the extra money.

Flying taught me a lot and I wanted my children to learn, too. Two female pilots came to me with a proposition to start a flying school for children between the ages of ten and sixteen. I went for the idea and the Boyne Flying Academy was born. Son John, at age twelve, was enrolled and loved it. Four years later he graduated, and at sixteen he soloed. I was quite proud, but the pride was short lived. John decided that he wanted to become an airline pilot. That announcement shocked the hell out of me. I wanted all of the kids to work for Boyne and eventually take over the business. Afraid that Stephen would get the same idea, I canceled the Air Academy right then! It took a bit of convincing, but John finally gave up his airline pilot ambition and now manages our western operations.

An airplane is one of the few luxuries I have. How can I put a price on what it has done for the company? Living in Boyne Falls, I never would have been able to conduct business in Montana, Utah or Washington. It would have meant getting up at 4:00 a.m. to catch the red eye, if there even is one, and driving to the airport, all of which takes longer than using the corporate airplane. Our 5,000 feet of runway at Boyne Mountain is not only useful to us, but it attracts other aircrafts which brings in hundreds of customers for skiing and golf.

In 1987, Kircher added a second Western resort to Boyne USA. This resort, located in Utah, truly positioned Boyne as a national skiing empire. Here he discusses how the deal originated, the factors which led to the purchase decision and the changes Boyne made to bring Brighton back into the black.

My Second Jackpot

You're indeed one of the lucky ones if you hit a jackpot once in your lifetime. Doing it twice is as likely as lightning hitting twice in the same place. But it happened to me. My first jackpot was the scenic chairlift my dad and I built in Gatlinburg, Tennessee, in 1953. The profits from that mother lode financed much of the development of Boyne Mountain and Boyne Highlands. It was a cash cow from the first year and even now it continues to subsidize the Boyne Mountain operation. The second jackpot is our Brighton, Utah, ski area 25 miles from Salt Lake City at the summit of Big Cottonwood Canyon.

It came about when my son, John, called me from Big Sky, saying he heard that the Brighton Ski Bowl might be for sale. John began extolling its virtues and potential. The ski area was at the summit of the Wasatch Mountain chain, the highest point in the range. It was blessed by snow you can't believe, with Brighton annually averaging 430 inches of the driest, lightest snow on earth — touted as "Champagne Powder" in the advertising of Utah ski areas.

Cold northwest winds flow over the warm waters of the Great Salt Lake, picking up moisture. The moisture is warmed by the hot sun as it is carried up to the higher 12,000-foot Wasatch Mountain elevations, with most of it wrung out from the clouds upon hitting the colder mountain air. This extremely dry precipitation falls primarily on Brighton and neighboring Alta ski area, with much of it missing Park City and neighboring areas located at lower altitudes, often forcing them to make snow. It's not unusual to have three or four feet of this fluffy, ultra-dry snow fall overnight on Brighton. It's so light you sink waist deep in it when you step outdoors. Scoop up a handful and you can blow it away with a puff. Snow like this is a ski operator's dream, and a powder skier's idea of heaven.

Another plus for Brighton, as John pointed out, was the proximity of Salt Lake City itself, a large, growing metropolis less than a half-hour's drive from the Brighton slopes. And for skiers who don't wish to drive and fight for scarce parking space, there's the Utah Transit Authority, an excellent, low-cost shuttle bus service that provides hourly round-trip transportation between Salt Lake City and the ski areas up the canyons.

I never enjoyed advantages like these at Boyne Mountain, Boyne Highlands or Big Sky, all three being hours away from populous cities. Nor did I have the luxury of a major airport like Salt Lake City's International at the back door. This busy airport is just 30 minutes driving time from Brighton and is serviced by a number of key airlines. The area's mountain, I discovered, had a variety of excellent terrain plus some very exhilarating runs for the black diamond and extreme skiers. The mountain also offered large areas of undeveloped terrain that could be opened up for slope expansion.

A big mountain, an abundance of snow, a population concentration only minutes away! Easy access! What more could a ski operator ask? John set up an appointment with the owners, the Doyle family. John, Art Tebo (our Chief Operations Officer) and I met with the Doyles to explore sale possibilities.

Brighton had been started by the senior Mr. Doyle and his sons at about the same time Norton, Christianson and I had started Boyne Mountain. After some penetrating investigation into the resort's history, the Doyle and Kircher families came to an agreement on price and other details, and Brighton Ski Bowl became part of Boyne USA in 1987. The two Doyle brothers, sons of the founder, stayed on and have done an excellent job managing the operation.

At the time we took over the area, Brighton lift tickets were priced at $5 per day. *Incredible! I charged that the day we opened the Mountain forty years earlier.* The owners of Solitude, the ski area directly below Brighton, and the Doyles had been in a price war. Neither had budged. Consequently, the rates were ridiculous, less than one-fourth that charged by nearby Park City, Deer Valley, Snowbird and other competition. That, of course, was one of the first things that had to be changed if this was to be the bonanza I thought it should be given all of the inherent advantages it possessed.

In taking over an established area you don't just jump in and hike rates overnight unless you're prepared to lose customers and take a lot of"bad guy" flack from the local media. You do it gradually, justifying your increases by improving facilities and amenities. By 1995 our lift ticket rates had been increased to $30 – still less than the rates charged by the major players in the Utah ski arena.

In reality, the Brighton jackpot took more than one pull of the handle for the royal flush to show up. It took over eight years, hard work and $17 million in investment in Brighton to get to that $30 level and provide the quality skiing experience I like to provide and skiers demand these days.

When Boyne took over Brighton, the food operation was privately owned and was dismal – housed in a run down building you wouldn't care to visit unless you were starving. We bought that out at an exorbitant price, through a forest service lease, tore down the ramshackle building, and built a handsome new cafeteria and skier's day lodge with rooms on the third floor able to accommodate 100 guests. The lodge included some sorely needed restrooms and an elevator for the third floor guests.

We got the forest service to approve new runs and we installed two high-speed quad detachable chairlifts, opened up four bowls, and bought out the privately owned ski rental operation, stocking it with the latest skis, boots and safety bindings. We also put in a modern sewage system. Previously, sewage had to be hauled out by tank truck to a disposal site in Salt Lake City.

Big Cottonwood Canyon is a narrow valley between encroaching mountains, similar to parts of the Colorado River winding between cliffs. Because of this, there's a limited amount of parking for autos and buses. We worked with the forest service and designed and built a modern bus terminal for the Transit Authority's buses and independent tour buses. Parking for private vehicles is still limited, and short of blasting out a mountain it always will be.

To get a jump on the season before the first major snow falls, we've put in snowmaking on 20% of the runs, equipped the resort with the latest groomers and tillers and enlarged the ski school. With Salt Lake City being so close we expanded night skiing, illuminating 270 acres, with more in the planning stage. Brighton now offers more night skiing than any resort in the Rockies.

When Boyne took over Brighton, it was the only ski area of the half-dozen or so nearby that allowed snowboarding. Most skiers hated snowboarders. Getting the two factions to coexist peaceably wasn't, and won't be, easy. Many of the young, cult-like "shredders" are rude, obnoxious, inconsiderate, reckless and dangerous. But they love Brighton and many skiing families appreciate the fact that the parents can ski while the kids "catch air" on other runs. Easing the situation is the fact that most snowboarders are in school during weekdays, leaving the slopes to downhillers except on weekends or when school is out.

I mulled the matter over countless weeks, finally deciding to keep things status quo as it had been when we took over the operation. It didn't take a rocket scientist's brain to convince me that snowboarding was the wave of the future, that it would grow faster than traditional downhill skiing. That was hammered home one day when I got a head count from the area manager. On that particular weekend we had sold about 10,000 lift tickets, with more than half of them bought by snowboarders. It was mostly kids in their teens from Salt Lake City who had grown up with skateboards. Never mind that they were already accomplished skiers. This was new. It was exciting. Something different. And they were taking to it in droves. I thought then and think now that the popularity of snowboarding is as unstoppable as giant waves in the ocean during a storm. And you go along or drown. (Even Stephen, my youngest son, has been caught up in the sport. Although he is an expert skier, he almost always takes his snowboard when he goes out to check Boyne slopes or have fun with friends. The rest of my kids are doing the same.)

We have permitted snowboarding at our other resorts for years. We built half-pipe courses for them — deep, long troughs gouged out of snow where they can "get air" and do their acrobatics. We have even sponsored national snowboarding tournaments that attract pros from around the country with the events being covered by national television.

It took Big Sky 15 years and over $50 million in improvements to show a profit. Brighton's balance sheet showed black ink after two years. In the 95/96 season we welcomed 400,000 customers to Brighton. The California market amounts to several hundred thousand skiers in the Salt Lake City area. When California gets good snow early we don't do as well, but a lean snow year in the Golden State means a fat year in Salt Lake.

The competition for the skiing dollar gets more fierce every year. While this is a concern, nearly fifty years of experience in the business tells me *give them quality and value and they will come.*

Chuck Moll was Kircher's right-hand man for over 40 years. Here, his wife remembers their life with Everett Kircher.

Through other eyes

Donna Moll

It was during the winter of 1946 that I met Everett Kircher. I was a freshman at Wayne State Detroit, and came to Hidden Valley with a family friend, Herman Geisert, for my first skiing experience. Everett, Jim Christianson, John Norton were some of the big skiers on the slopes, and I was the young kid who tagged along – just surviving on hills that they had mastered. I listened to Everett's visionary ideas of a greater ski development in the are, and I was thrilled to see the new Boyne Maountain lodge in 1949, and to ski the first winter on the Pierson Trail and Hemlock. Anyone who skied that slope had to manually pack it first, however. It was exciting enough for me to want to live in the area, so I accepted a teaching position for $2,700.00 in Boyne City High School in June 1949.

Chuck Moll, a graduate of Michigan State in hotel management, and recently returned from World War II as a First Lieutenant, was managing a small summer resort on Walloon Lake: Shadow Trails Inn. We met, courted and were married in 1950. Boyne was looking for a new manager, and Everett and Chuck began their 40 year Boyne experience together in 1950. Chuck and Everett worked seven days a week when Boyne was open for business. A day off was not on their agenda. One of our four children commented to him, "Dad, I'd like to see you sometime in the daylight."

The relationship between Everett and Chuck, both business and personal, was refered to by many people as "the perfect marriage." Everett was the person with the ideas, vision and courage to take the risk, and Chuck was the person who made them work. Each personality was strong, yet opposite. They shared similar values and directions. Between them, they fought battles and together they fought battles.

As Boyne grew and expanded, Chuck played a major role with Everett in the purchases and building of Boyne USA.

After Chuck retired at 65 in 1984, and Art Tebo stepped into his position as General Manager of Boyne USA Enterprises, Chuck's workaholic nature could not separate his Boyne attachment from his life. For several years he found his way back to the corporate offices, and even for a few hours a day his presence and impact continued to be valuable. Chuck and Everett were close, and they were often found at the driving range, or on the golf course discussing one of Boyne's latest challenges.

Chuck's 11 years of retirement with home life, travels and winters in Florida did not lessen his pride, loyalty and love for Boyne USA – nor for his employer and best friend Everett Kircher.

Boyne USA has experienced considerable growth since Kircher started the small, midwestern resort, Boyne Ski Lodge, Inc., in the 1947-48 season. Each advancement was taken slowly, after being carefully calculated by Kircher, his family and his staff. After adding golf courses, scenic chairlifts, and, of course, ski resorts across the country, what could be next for Boyne?

Bay Harbor

The Journey Continues

At times it feels as if Norton, Christianson and myself started Boyne just yesterday. And at other times it seems like every bit of the fifty years it's been. Not one of us would have ever guessed in 1947 that Boyne Ski Lodge, Inc. could have transformed into five major year-round resorts, golf courses from Montana to Florida and even a scenic chairlift in Tennessee. It's been a lot of work – but also a lot of fun.

Each time we grew, it started with a common event – a phone call. When we needed the money to develop Boyne Mountain, the call came from Mr. Maples in Tennessee asking me to build him a chairlift. As you know, I built it for myself and the money from it sure helped us get the ball rolling. Then, as we established Boyne, other calls came in. "Hey, did you hear? There's a resort in Montana for sale. It's called Big Sky." Or, "A place in Utah is up… are you interested?"

We took dozens of trips to resorts across the country to inspect them and see if we were interested in making a purchase. I'm very proud of the selections we've added to the Boyne family – they all truly provide the "Boyne" experience. For example, our latest addition, Crystal Mountain, is located in Washington, with Mt. Rainier as its backdrop. We immediately added a new 6-place, high-speed chairlift, the first in the Northwest, and upgraded other skiing services. We're also looking into expanding terrain. All of these changes make it a better ski resort and therefore, part of the Boyne family.

I'm also very proud of the other accomplishments of Boyne USA – the patented Highlands Snow Gun, the advancements in up-hill travel and the expansion into summer business such as golf. All have helped us develop the very finest facilities in the industry.

Our latest venture into golf, Bay Harbor Golf Club, is our most extensive yet – and will be the envy of the Midwest. Located on Lake Michigan between Petoskey and Charlevoix, the course is already rated as one of the best in the country. The holes along the bluffs of Lake Michigan are truly beautiful.

So beautiful, in fact, that Bay Harbor G.C. was selected to host Shell's Wonderful World of Golf in September, 1998. This is a very prestigious event that has been played at exotic locations all over the world by many of golf's legends. In the event at Bay Harbor, Tom Lehman and Phil Mickelson will compete for $150,000 in prize money on the Links and Quarry courses.

In addition to the golf course, we will own and operate the Inn at Bay Harbor G.C. which is set to be completed this year (1998). It's reminiscent of the grand resort hotels that used to decorate this area. My son Stephen, who has headed up the Bay Harbor project, describes the Inn as '19th century charm with 21st century technology.'

Today, my family and the rest of Boyne's Board of Directors run the majority of operations at all of our resorts. My sons, John and Stephen, run our Western and Midwestern Operations, while daughters Amy and Kathryn manage the Boyne South golf course and Boyne Design Group. I stay involved, though, often making sure they are thinking straight.

Although I am suffering from failing kidneys and am forced to undergo kidney dialysis several times a week, I remain active in the ongoing business of Boyne USA. And I plan on sticking around for a while, especially to make sure that all the plans that are in the works get completed.

For example, in addition to the 188-room condominium hotel and conference center being built at Bay Harbor, we are building a 200-room condo hotel at Boyne Mountain and a 235-room facility at Big Sky. We are also adding two high-speed quads at Brighton before the 2002 Winter Olympics are held at Salt Lake City. All of this should keep my kids busy and out of mischief while I also pursue the possibility of a kidney transplant.

People frequently ask me where Boyne, USA will go next – what resort or sport will we grow into in the future. I don't know for sure, just as I wasn't sure fifty years ago that there was a future in the ski business for me. But I am sure of one thing – as long as we make smart decisions, the phone will continue to ring and opportunities will be available.

This game ain't over…it's just beginning.

A publicity promotion at Big Sky.

The most famous view of Big Sky.

A lone skier tests his mettle.

Kircher enjoys the contradiction of his father's 1927 Ford
Model T and his modern mode of transport.

Explorer double chairlift approaches the lodge at Big Sky.

Our skiers enjoy the powder-experience out west.

A snowboarder leaves his signature carve
on the mountain.

Hole #18 at the Monument.

Quarry #17 at Bay Harbor G.C.

#18 on the Heather Highlands.

#11 Alpine at Boyne Mountain.

#15 on the Moor course at Boyne Highlands.

Bay Harbor G.C. #1 hole-Links course.

Bay Harbor G.C. #7-Links course.

Michigan Living magazine cover featuring Everett and
Steve Kircher, 1993.

Everett and Clayton Watson, the director of Gatlinburg, 1997.